EASY DOG TREATS COOKBOOK

*The Best Way to Reward Your Dog with Love and Nutrition
with More Than 80 Homemade Healthy & Delicious Dog Treats Recipes*

TIMI FOSTER

CONTENTS

DISCLAIMER

This cookbook is designed to provide tasty and healthy treat recipes for dogs. However, it is important to remember that treats should never make up more than 10% of your dog's daily diet. Overfeeding can lead to health issues, including overweight and nutritional imbalances.

We strongly advise consulting with a veterinarian or a qualified animal nutritionist before making any significant changes to your dog's diet, especially in the case of puppies, senior dogs, and dogs with specific dietary or health needs. Every dog is unique and may have individual nutritional requirements.

The recipes in this book are intended to be used as occasional treats and should not replace a balanced and complete diet. The use of these recipes is at the owner's discretion and should always be overseen by an animal health professional.

Remember: the health and well-being of your dog are the top priority. Make informed and conscious decisions to ensure that your four-legged friend remains happy, healthy, and properly nourished.

INTRODUCTION

Welcome to a world where dogs are more than just pets; they're cherished members of our family. In this book, we're going to explore the joyful art of making treats for our furry friends - because they deserve the best!

Treating our dogs isn't just about spoiling them; it's a wonderful way to bond, train, and share love. Whether it's a reward for good behavior, an aid in moments of anxiety, or just a way to say "I love you," these treats do so much more than fill their bellies.

You'll find a collection of unique, easy, and scrumptious recipes here. These are perfect for everyday rewards or for those times when you want to give your pup something extra special. Us dog lovers know that treats are an essential part of how we communicate with our pets. They help in training, provide comfort during anxious times, and strengthen our bond.

Training and Positive Reinforcement

Let's talk about training and positive reinforcement. Whether it's a hearty "Good job!" or their favorite snack, the right treat can make learning new tricks and good behavior fun and effective. This book includes a special section, a little bonus, if you will, about using treats wisely in training. Did you know dogs learn much quicker with rewards than with punishments? That's where these yummy treats come in!

Distraction and Alleviation of Anxiety

Our furry pals can get anxious too, and this is where treats can be real game-changers. They're great for distracting your dog during stressful times like visits to the vet or grooming sessions. And for high-energy dogs, chewy treats can be a fantastic way to keep them busy and calm. It's all about turning anxious energy into positive vibes.

Bonding and Emotion

Every treat you give is a little message of love, helping to strengthen that beautiful bond you share. Those moments of close connection, shared happiness, and mutual understanding come through these homemade creations. The treats in this book aren't just tasty; they're little tokens of affection that can make your dog feel loved, valued, and an integral part of your family.

Celebration and Special Occasions

And who doesn't love a celebration? Birthdays, adoption days, holidays - every occasion is a chance to make your dog feel extra special. These treats are perfect for adding a bit of festivity and making memories together. Whether it's marking a milestone or just bringing a bit of extra joy to their day, these goodies will be a highlight of celebrating life with your furry best friend.

In this book, we're going to dive into why homemade treats are not only fun but also incredibly rewarding to make. So, let's get started and whip up some tail-wagging goodness!

Welcome to a world where dogs are more than just pets; they're cherished members of our family. In this book, we're going to explore the joyful art of making treats for our furry friends - because they deserve the best!

Treating our dogs isn't just about spoiling them; it's a wonderful way to bond, train, and share love. Whether it's a reward for good behavior, an aid in moments of anxiety, or just a way to say "I love you," these treats do so much more than fill their bellies.

You'll find a collection of unique, easy, and scrumptious recipes here. These are perfect for everyday rewards or for those times when you want to give your pup something extra special. Us dog lovers know that treats are an essential part of how we communicate with our pets. They help in training, provide comfort during anxious times, and strengthen our bond.

Training and Positive Reinforcement

Let's talk about training and positive reinforcement. Whether it's a hearty "Good job!" or their favorite snack, the right treat can make learning new tricks and good behavior fun and effective. This book includes a special section, a little bonus, if you will, about using treats wisely in training. Did you know dogs learn much quicker with rewards than with punishments? That's where these yummy treats come in!

Distraction and Alleviation of Anxiety

Our furry pals can get anxious too, and this is where treats can be real game-changers. They're great for distracting your dog during stressful times like visits to the vet or grooming sessions. And for high-energy dogs, chewy treats can be a fantastic way to keep them busy and calm. It's all about turning anxious energy into positive vibes.

Bonding and Emotion

Every treat you give is a little message of love, helping to strengthen that beautiful bond you share. Those moments of close connection, shared happiness, and mutual understanding come through these homemade creations. The treats in this book aren't just tasty; they're little tokens of affection that can make your dog feel loved, valued, and an integral part of your family.

Celebration and Special Occasions

And who doesn't love a celebration? Birthdays, adoption days, holidays - every occasion is a chance to make your dog feel extra special. These treats are perfect for adding a bit of festivity and making memories together. Whether it's marking a milestone or just bringing a bit of extra joy to their day, these goodies will be a highlight of celebrating life with your furry best friend.

In this book, we're going to dive into why homemade treats are not only fun but also incredibly rewarding to make. So, let's get started and whip up some tail-wagging goodness!

5 GREAT REASONS TO MAKE HOMEMADE TREATS

In the market, as we well know, there are many varieties of dog treats, snacks, and bites... but when you choose to make them at home, you can be completely sure that the ingredients are of high quality, and you can avoid specific allergies and intolerances while also saving money and preventing boredom from having to settle for the same taste every day.

Preparing homemade treats can be a fun activity to do as a family, even involving children with molds and cutters. However, as enjoyable as it can be to do during a carefree afternoon, it is always necessary to keep in mind that not all food edible for us is also good for them; preparing treats for our dogs with love requires close attention and safe recipes. On this topic, I have dedicated an important chapter that you will find before the recipe section, which I recommend you read carefully.

But first, let's see the 5 good reasons why dedicating yourself to homemade preparation is a really good idea:

Knowing Exactly What's In Them
When you're the chef, you know exactly what's going into those treats. No hidden nasties here! You can skip those additives, preservatives, and fillers that often sneak into store-bought treats. Instead, you get to use fresh, natural ingredients that are just right for your pooch's health.

Safety and Recalls? Not a Worry!
Homemade means you're not sweating over those scary recalls due to contamination or unsafe ingredients. You'll have peace of mind knowing your treats are safe, made in a clean kitchen by the best chef in town – you!

Easy on the Wallet
Guess what? Making treats at home can be kinder to your budget. Those store-bought options can be pricey (and sometimes come with less-than-eco-friendly packaging). Bulk cooking not only saves time but also cuts down the cost big time!

Tailored Tastes and Nutrition
Got a picky eater or a dog with special dietary needs? No problem! You can customize these treats to suit their taste buds and nutritional requirements. Want to add in some superfoods or go grain-free or high-protein? You've got it! Plus, you can adjust for any allergies or sensitivities. Think pumpkin, sweet potatoes, or omega-rich oils – yummy and healthy!

Family Fun and Bonding Time
Making dog treats can be a blast for the whole family! Get the kids involved in the kitchen and teach them about caring for pets. It's a beautiful way to bond, create shared experiences, and instill a sense of responsibility and love for animals.

Homemade treats are a concentrate of love, a tangible expression of your friendship, demonstrating a deeper level of care and commitment to the health and happiness of your dog.

BALANCING TREATS IN A HEALTHY DIET

Incorporating treats into a dog's diet requires a strategic approach to ensure that they truly contribute to their overall health. While regular dog food constitutes the basis of daily nutritional intake, treats play a supplementary role. However, this does not mean that their nutritional value should be neglected. Treats should be seen as an extension of a dog's diet, providing not only pleasure but also essential nutrients of good quality.

The key is always to maintain a good balance: treats should complement the regular diet, filling any nutritional gaps and never compromising the overall nutritional integrity of the diet. This requires careful selection of treats based on their ingredients and nutritional content. A handy tip? Keep the treat calories to less than 10% of your doggy's daily needs to keep everything in check.

Indeed, it's imperative to not forget that treats can contribute to weight gain and for this reason, we can't avoid considering their calories. Healthier treats have a lower caloric count and preparing them at home allows for further dietary customization: recipes can be chosen or adapted to meet the specific needs or restrictions of your dog. Whether it's low-fat, grain-free, or high-protein treats, you can modify the recipes to meet your pet's unique needs, making them an ideal option even if your dog has allergies or specific sensitivities.

Healthy treats can be an effective tool for training, and choosing to use small, low-calorie options helps to prevent overfeeding even during long or frequent training sessions. In any case, if a dog has consumed a high amount of treats on a given day, it might be wise to slightly reduce the portion of their regular meal to maintain a balanced caloric intake.

Treats are more than a little indulgence; they're a key part of your dog's diet and your bond. By choosing or whipping up healthy treats, you're not just filling their tummy; you're nourishing their health and showing your love.

Moderation is the magic word here – it's all about making sure those treats fit perfectly into a diet that's just right for your pup. It's a lovely way to say 'I love you' and keep them healthy!

UNDERSTANDING DOG TREAT LABELS

So, you can't always make homemade treats for your furry friend? That's absolutely okay! We all have those busy weeks or even longer stretches when whipping up something extra isn't possible. And sometimes, it's just more convenient to grab a pack of treats, especially when you're on the go, traveling, or in the middle of training sessions. That's why I've included a friendly guide in this book to help you pick the best commercial treats for your dog, ensuring they're just as loved even with store-bought goodies.

Wading through the sea of dog treats on the market can seem overwhelming, right? But understanding what those labels are really saying is key to making sure your pup gets only the best. Learning to read these is like learning a new language of love for your pet.

Commercial dog treat labels can be complex, often filled with a long list of ingredients and nutritional information that can seem overwhelming. Here are some things to look into:

Ingredient list: Ingredients are listed in order by weight, so the first few items are what make up most of the treat. Keep your eyes peeled for high-quality proteins like chicken, beef, or fish topping that list. Be wary of products where grains or by-products are at the top, as they are often used as fillers for cost savings.

Warning signs on labels: Some ingredients are red flags. Artificial colors and flavors, preservatives like BHA and BHT, and vague terms like "meat meal" or "animal fat" are not what you want for your pup. They're the not-so-good stuff, often found in lower-quality treats.
Compare different brands and types of treats. Look for those with the highest quality ingredients and the fewest additives. Almost always, the shorter and simpler the ingredient list, the better.

Nutrition know-how: Consider your dog's specific nutritional needs. For example, older dogs may benefit from treats that support joint health, while overweight dogs may require low-calorie options.
In addition, quality snacks can contain very beneficial supplements, vitamins, and minerals.

Transparency equals trust: Opt for brands that are transparent regarding their sourcing and production processes. Brands that provide detailed information about their ingredients and where they come from are generally more reliable. A simple online search can reveal which companies are really doing responsible and ethical work.

Marketing traps: Be wary of marketing tricks. Terms like "gourmet" or "premium" are not regulated and can be misleading. Focus on the ingredient list and nutritional information rather than persuasive packaging.

Ask for advice: If you're ever unsure, your vet is your go-to. They can guide you based on your dog's health, breed, age, and specific dietary needs.

Always opt for quality over quantity, treats are a supplement to your dog's diet and should be chosen with the same care as their regular food.

CHOOSING THE BEST INGREDIENTS

When we decide to make our dog's treats, the goal is to wrap our love for their health and joy in every bite. So, let's get into the heart of making super nutritious and delicious treats for our furry pals!

In our dogs' diet, whether it's their regular meals or treats, here's what should never be missing:

High-Quality Proteins

Proteins are the cornerstone of a healthy diet for dogs. They are vital for muscle growth, tissue repair, and overall well-being. Generally, the most used animal proteins are those contained in chicken, beef, lamb, fish, or turkey meat. These are complete protein sources that contain all the essential amino acids that dogs need. For dogs with specific allergies or dietary needs, less common meats such as kangaroo, deer, bison, rabbit, venison are also recommended.

Plant-based ingredients also contain good proteins, assimilable by our dogs and equally useful and beneficial that we can include in our recipes.

Beneficial Fats

Fats are a crucial source of energy for dogs and help in the absorption of nutrients. They also help maintain a healthy skin and coat.

- Omega fatty acids: Ingredients like fish oil, flaxseed, or chia seeds are excellent sources of omega-3 and omega-6 fatty acids, promoting a shiny coat and healthy skin.
- Healthy oils: Coconut oil and olive oil are not only good sources of fats, but they also have anti-inflammatory properties.

Carbohydrates and Fibers

Although dogs do not have a strict requirement for carbohydrates, they can be a beneficial part of their diet, providing energy and aiding digestive health.

- Whole grains: Brown rice, barley, and oats are good sources of carbohydrates that also offer fiber, vitamins, and minerals.
- Fruits and vegetables: Carrots, apples, blueberries, pumpkin, and sweet potatoes provide natural sugars, fiber, and essential nutrients.

Vitamins and Minerals

A balanced diet must include the right vitamins and minerals to support overall health.

- Fruits and vegetables: These not only provide natural fibers but are also rich in essential vitamins and antioxidants. For example, blueberries are rich in antioxidants, while spinach offers iron and vitamin K.

Probiotics and Prebiotics

Gut health is fundamental for the overall well-being of our dogs, and maintaining the right balance of intestinal flora is essential.

- Natural sources: Ingredients like yogurt or fermented vegetables can be good sources of probiotics, while prebiotics can be found in ingredients like sweet potato.

While when it comes to fully feeding our dogs with homemade food it is essential to consider the right balance between various nutrients and to study the subject in depth, as far as treats are concerned, even those with no experience can get involved without fret. It will be enough to keep in mind the importance of the quality of raw materials and correct administration without excesses in addition to the aspects we have talked about in the previous chapters.

However, if at this moment you are considering switching entirely to a homemade diet, starting to produce treats yourself, while studying the broader subject, can be an excellent start.

WHAT TO USE AND WHAT TO AVOID

Numerous ingredients are perfectly safe for your furry companion. Among the favorites for dogs are foods like carrots, both white and brown rice, buckwheat, quinoa, plain yogurt without any added sweeteners, salmon, various types of fish, all kinds of meat, blueberries, bananas, cucumbers, apples (making sure to remove the core), seedless watermelon, beetroots, pumpkin, and broccoli.

It's also widely known that chocolate is extremely toxic to dogs and the severity of the reaction often depends on the quantity consumed. However, it's important to note that there are certain, maybe even lesser-known foods where even a small amount can be critically harmful. The upcoming section will present an in-depth overview of the top 10 food items that are highly dangerous and should always be kept away from dogs.

TOP 10 TOXIC INGREDIENTS

Alcohol – Just like in humans, even a small amount of alcohol can harm a dog's brain and liver. Dogs are often attracted to the taste and smell of beer, so it's important to keep it, and all alcoholic drinks, away from them.

Avocado – Avocado contains a fungicidal toxin called persin, which is harmless to humans but highly toxic to dogs. Consuming avocados, including their leaves, bark, and fruit, can lead to vomiting and diarrhea in dogs. The large seed poses an additional risk if swallowed, potentially causing blockages in the stomach or intestines, which can be fatal.

Chocolate – Most are aware that chocolate is harmful to dogs, primarily due to theobromine, an alkaloid found in cacao beans. Present in all types of chocolate, in large quantities, it can damage a dog's heart and nervous system. Symptoms of chocolate poisoning include vomiting, diarrhea, and hyperactivity.

Coffee & Tea – As they contain caffeine, coffee and tea can be deadly for dogs; even coffee beans are dangerous. Immediate veterinary care is advised if a dog consumes caffeine.

Grapes & Raisins – Despite some dogs seemingly being able to eat grapes without issue, it's purely luck. Grapes and raisins can cause kidney failure in dogs, and even small amounts can lead to continuous vomiting and lethargy.

Macadamia Nuts – Ingesting even small amounts of macadamia nuts can be deadly for dogs. Symptoms of poisoning include vomiting, fever, and seizures, so it's crucial to keep these nuts and foods containing them away from dogs.

Onions and Garlic – All forms of onions and garlic are highly toxic to dogs, as they can destroy red blood cells and lead to anemia. Foods containing powdered versions are also dangerous. Vomiting and breathing difficulties are early symptoms of poisoning.

Peach and Plum Pits – The pits of peaches and plums contain cyanide, toxic to both humans and dogs. If ingested by dogs, cyanide release can be fatal within minutes, with signs including excessive salivation, breathing difficulties, paralysis, and a rapid heartbeat.

Unbaked Yeast Dough – Fresh yeast dough, like that used in donuts, should not be given to dogs. It rises in warm environments, including a dog's stomach, stretching it painfully.

Xylitol or Birch Sugar – Artificial sweeteners, particularly xylitol, can cause liver failure in dogs within days. Symptoms include lethargy, vomiting, coordination problems, and seizures. Keeping xylitol-rich foods out of dogs' reach is essential.

ALTERNATIVES FOR ALLERGY CONCERNS

While most recipes in this book are suitable for dogs with common allergies, here you will find some alternatives to replace certain ingredients if your dog is particularly sensitive or has specific dietary needs. Remember, it's important, especially in the case of dogs with allergies or particular health problems, to always consult with your veterinarian before introducing significant changes to your pets' diet.

Butter Alternatives
- Coconut oil
- Fish oil
- Olive oil
- Peanut oil

Egg Alternatives
- 1 ripe banana, mashed, replaces 1 egg.
- 1 tablespoon of unsweetened applesauce replaces 1 egg.
- Boil 1/4 cup of flaxseed flour in 3/4 cup of water for 5-7 minutes or until thick.
  Use 4 tablespoons for 1 egg.
- Mix 1 tablespoon of chia seeds with 3 tablespoons of water.
  Let it sit for 7-10 minutes to form a gel to replace 1 egg.

Milk Alternatives
- Unsweetened coconut milk
- Unsweetened almond milk
- Water

Yogurt Alternative
- Coconut milk yogurt
- Almond milk yogurt

Wheat Flour Alternatives
- Almond flour
- Coconut flour
- Rice flour

To make recipe selection easier and allow for convenient navigation within the book, I have created two indexes located at the end of the book:

- An **ALPHABETICAL INDEX OF INGREDIENTS,** which enables you to choose a recipe based on what you already have at home.
- A **RECIPE CATEGORY INDEX,** which covers preparation methods, specific dietary needs, and even health benefits for your dog.

<u>Here is the legend of symbols I have used to organize all the recipes:</u>

Meat-Based Treats

Fish-Based Treats

Vegetarian Treats

NO-Bake Treats

Frozen Treats

Training Treats

Low-Fat & Low-Calories Treats

Dental & Oral Care Treats

Treats for Sensitive Dog

Chews & Stress Relief

Super Food & Nutrient Treats

Special Occasion Sweets & Treats

Baking Silicon Mats Treats

IMPORTANT INGREDIENT NOTE

When preparing homemade treats for your dog, it's crucial to use ingredients that are safe and healthy for them. Please pay special attention to the following guidelines to ensure the well-being of your furry friend:

- **Whole Grains and Flours:** Opt for whole grains like oatmeal, brown rice flour, or barley flour. These are healthier options for dogs compared to bleached or processed flours. Avoid using flours that may contain even just traces of gluten if your dog is sensitive or allergic to it.

- **Peanut Butter:** Always use xylitol-free peanut butter. Xylitol is a common sweetener in human foods and is extremely toxic to dogs, even in small amounts. Always read the label.

- **Parsley:** Use only curly parsley in these recipes. Italian (flat) parsley can be toxic to dogs. If you're unsure which one you have, it's best to omit it entirely from the recipe to be safe.

- **Broth:** When using broth in recipes, ensure it does not include onions or garlic. It's also recommendable to use low-sodium (or no sodium, if available). Always check the ingredients list of the broth to confirm it's free from these elements.

- **Healthy Fats:** Incorporate healthy fats like coconut oil or flaxseed oil. Avoid using fats that are high in saturated fats or any hydrogenated oils.

- **Dairy Products:** Almost all dogs are lactose intolerant, so use dairy products cautiously. Plain, unsweetened yogurt and low-lactose cheeses can be used in small quantities if your dog can digest them well, but for best results, avoid dairy products altogether.

- **Sweeteners:** Avoid using any artificial sweeteners. If you need to sweeten a recipe, a small amount of natural sweeteners like honey can be used sparingly. Remember, treats do not need to be overly sweet.

- **Water Content:** If using canned vegetables or fruits, opt for those without added salt or sugar. Also, be wary of the water content in fruits and vegetables, as too much can make treats soggy.

By following these guidelines, you can create delicious and healthy treats that are safe for your beloved pet. Remember, treats should be given in moderation and are not a substitute for a balanced diet.

MEAT-BASED DELIGHTS

If you're a fan of savory flavors, you're going to adore this section!
Get ready to whip up some scrumptious meat-based treats that your four-legged companion will drool over. You'll see it's surprisingly easy to do!
Packed with high-quality proteins, these treats are not just tasty but also incredibly healthy for your pooch.

CHICKEN LOVER TREAT

Ingredients:

- 5.6 oz whole wheat flour (160 g)
- 3.5 oz chicken heart (100 g)
- 1.7 oz chicken liver (50 g)
- 2 medium eggs
- 1/4 tsp rosehip powder (optional)

Preparation:

1. Prepare ingredients at room temperature.
2. Preheat the oven to 338 F (170° C), line the baking tray with parchment paper.
3. Clean, then dice liver and heart into big chunks.
4. Mix the ingredients with the food blender to get a homogeneous "dough". Adjust amounts if needed.
5. Spread the mixture on the baking tray.
6. Bake for approximately 20 minutes, until golden brown.
7. Break or cut into pieces.
8. Store in an airtight container or put them in the freezer to make them last longer.

Nutrition Facts:
(Analytical components in 3.5 oz)

- **Recipe's kcal** — **221 kcal**
- Fat — 5.6 g
- Carbohydrate — 27.7 g
- Fiber — 4.2 g
- Protein — 16.9 g

BEEF DOG TREAT

Ingredients:

- 7 oz ground beef (cooked) (200 g)
- 3.2 oz buckwheat (cooked) (90 g)
- 0.4 oz oat flour (10 g)
- 1 medium egg
- 1/4 tsp rosehip powder (optional)

Preparation:

1. Prepare ingredients at room temperature.
2. Preheat the oven to 356 F (180° C), line the baking tray with parchment paper.
3. Mash cooked buckwheat with a fork.
4. Mix the ingredients in a bowl to get a homogeneous "dough". Adjust amounts if needed.
5. Spoon the batter into muffin tin or oven-safe silicone mold.
6. Bake for approximately 20 minutes, until golden brown.
7. Put them on a rack to cool completely.
8. Store in an airtight container or put them in the freezer to make them last longer.

Nutrition Facts:
(Analytical components in 3.5 oz)

- **Recipe's kcal** — **302 kcal**
- Fat — 11.2 g
- Carbohydrate — 7.1 g
- Fiber — 0.9 g
- Protein — 18 g

LAMB DOG TREAT

Ingredients:

- 7 oz ground lamb (cooked) (200 g)
- 3.2 oz buckwheat (cooked) (90 g)
- 0.4 oz oat flour (10 g)
- 1 medium egg
- 1/4 tsp rosehip powder (optional)

Preparation:

1. Prepare ingredients at room temperature.
2. Preheat the oven to 356 F (180° C), line the baking tray with parchment paper.
3. Mash cooked buckwheat with a fork.
4. Mix the ingredients in a bowl to get a homogeneous "dough". Adjust amounts if needed.
5. Spoon the batter into muffin tin or oven-safe silicone mold.
6. Bake for approximately 20 minutes, until golden brown.
7. Put them on a rack to cool completely.
8. Store in an airtight container or put them in the freezer to make them last longer.

Nutrition Facts:
(Analytical components in 3.5 oz)

- **Recipe's kcal**   **222 kcal**
- Fat   13.9 g
- Carbohydrate   7.1 g
- Fiber   0.9 g
- Protein   16.4 g

LAMB & CARROT TREAT

Ingredients:

- 7 oz brown rice flour (200 g)
- 3.5 oz lamb (cooked, mashed) (100 g)
- 3.5 oz carrot (cooked, mashed) (100 g)
- 3 medium eggs
- 1/4 tsp rosehip powder (optional)

Preparation:

1. Prepare ingredients at room temperature.
2. Preheat the oven to 365 F (185° C), line the baking tray with parchment paper.
3. Beat the eggs, then mix the ingredients in a bowl to get a homogeneous "dough". Adjust amounts if needed.
4. Spread the mixture evenly on the baking tray, and bake for 30-40 minutes, until golden brown.
5. Put on a rack to cool completely. Break into pieces.
6. Store in an airtight container or put them in the freezer to make them last longer.

Nutrition Facts:
(Analytical components in 3.5 oz)

- **Recipe's kcal**   **214 kcal**
- Fat   6.8 g
- Carbohydrate   29.4 g
- Fiber   2.3 g
- Protein   9.7 g

CHEDDAR & BACON DELIGHTS

Ingredients:

- 1 1/2 cups rolled oats (120 g)
- 1/2 cup shredded cheddar cheese (55 g)
- 4 strips bacon, cooked and crumbled
- 2 medium eggs

Nutrition Facts:
(Analytical components in 3.5 oz)

Recipe's kcal	214 kcal
Fat	6.8 g
Carbohydrate	29.4 g
Fiber	2.3 g
Protein	9.7 g

Preparation:

1. Preheat your oven to 350°F (175°C).
2. In the bowl of a food processor, combine the rolled oats, shredded cheddar cheese, and crumbled bacon. Process these ingredients until they achieve a crumb-like consistency.
3. To the food processor, add two eggs. Continue to process until the mixture forms into a sticky dough.
4. Lightly sprinkle either flour or finely ground oats onto a wooden cutting board. Roll the dough out to about ¼-inch thickness.
5. Using a cookie cutter, cut out the dough into your desired shapes for the treats.
6. Place the cut-out dog treats on a baking sheet lined with parchment paper. Bake in the preheated oven for 20 minutes.
7. Allow the treats to cool completely. Once cooled, store them in an airtight glass or plastic container.

PEANUT BUTTER BACON DOG TREATS

Ingredients:

- 1 cup peanut butter (250 g) (Xylitol-free peanut butter)
- 3/4 cup rice milk (180 ml)
- 1 large egg
- 2 cups whole-wheat flour (spooned & leveled) (250 g)
- 1 tbsp baking powder
- 1/3 cup rolled oats (30 g)
- 2–3 strips cooked bacon, chopped

Nutrition Facts:
(Analytical components in 3.5 oz)

Recipe's kcal	302 kcal
Fat	11.2 g
Carbohydrate	7.1 g
Fiber	0.9 g
Protein	18 g

Preparation:

1. Preheat the oven to 325°F (163°C). Line two large baking sheets with parchment paper or silicone baking mats. Set aside.
2. In a large bowl, mix the peanut butter, rise milk, and egg with a wooden spoon or silicone spatula. Add the flour and baking powder, mixing well. You may need to use your hands on a floured surface for this step. Mix in the oats and bacon to the dough, which will be thick and heavy.
3. On a floured surface, roll out the dough with a floured rolling pin. Cut into shapes using a 3-inch cookie cutter (or any size you prefer). Arrange the treats on the prepared baking sheets.
4. Bake the treats for 18-20 minutes or until lightly browned on the bottom. Then flip them and bake for an additional 10-12 minutes.
5. Allow the treats to cool completely before serving. Store leftovers at room temperature for up to 1 week or in the refrigerator for up to 2 weeks.

FISH-BASED DELIGHTS

If the ocean's bounty is what excites your palate, you'll be thrilled with the 'Fish-Based Delights' section! Here, you'll discover how to create mouth-watering treats for your furry friend, using the best of what the sea has to offer. Loaded with beneficial oils, omega-3 fatty acids, and lean proteins, these fish-based treats are a fantastic way to boost your dog's health.

TUNA DOG TREAT

Ingredients:

- 7 oz tuna (cooked) (200 g)
- 3.2 oz buckwheat (cooked) (90 g)
- 0.4 oz oat flour (10 g)
- 1 medium egg
- 1/4 tsp rosehip powder (optional)

Preparation:

1. Prepare ingredients at room temperature.
2. Preheat the oven to 356 F (180° C), line the baking tray with parchment paper.
3. Mash cooked buckwheat with a fork.
4. Mix the ingredients in a bowl to get a homogeneous "dough". Adjust amounts if needed.
5. Spoon the batter into muffin tin or oven-safe silicone mold.
6. Bake for approximately 20 minutes, until golden brown.
7. Put them on a rack to cool completely.
8. Store in an airtight container or put them in the freezer to make them last longer.

Nutrition Facts:
(Analytical components in 3.5 oz)

Recipe's kcal	**173 kcal**
Fat	8.9 g
Carbohydrate	7.1 g
Fiber	0.9 g
Protein	15.8 g

SALMON & PUMPKIN DOG TREAT

Ingredients:

- 7 oz brown rice flour (200 g)
- 3.5 oz salmon (cooked, mashed (100 g)
- 3.5 oz pumpkin (cooked, mashed (100 g)
- 3 medium eggs
- 1/4 tsp rosehip powder (optional)

Preparation:

1. Prepare ingredients at room temperature.
2. Preheat the oven to 365 F (185° C), line the baking tray with parchment paper.
3. Beat the eggs, then mix the ingredients in a bowl to get a homogeneous "dough". Adjust amounts if needed.
4. Spread the mixture evenly on the baking tray, and bake for 30-40 minutes, until golden brown.
5. Put on a rack to cool completely.
6. Store in an airtight container or put them in the freezer to make them last longer.

Nutrition Facts:
(Analytical components in 3.5 oz)

Recipe's kcal	**201 kcal**
Fat	5.1 g
Carbohydrate	27.9 g
Fiber	1.9 g
Protein	9.1 g

TUNA & CARROT DOG TREAT

Ingredients:

- 7 oz brown rice flour (200 g)
- 3.5 oz tuna (cooked, mashed) (100 g)
- 3.5 oz carrot (cooked, mashed (100 g)
- 3 medium eggs
- 1/4 tsp rosehip powder (optional)

Preparation:

1. Prepare ingredients at room temperature.
2. Preheat the oven to 365 F (185° C), line the baking tray with parchment paper.
3. Beat the eggs, then mix the ingredients in a bowl to get a homogeneous "dough". Adjust amounts if needed.
4. Spread the mixture evenly on the baking tray, and bake for 30-40 minutes, until golden brown.
5. Put on a rack to cool completely.
6. Store in an airtight container or put them in the freezer to make them last longer.

Nutrition Facts:
(Analytical components in 3.5 oz)

Recipe's kcal	**203 kcal**
Fat	5.1 g
Carbohydrate	29.4 g
Fiber	2.3 g
Protein	9.1 g

SALMON & CARROT DOG TREAT

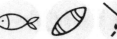

Ingredients:

- 7 oz brown rice flour (200 g)
- 3.5 oz salmon (cooked, mashed) (100 g)
- 3.5 oz carrot (cooked, mashed) (100 g)
- 3 medium eggs
- 1/4 tsp rosehip powder (optional)

Preparation:

1. Prepare ingredients at room temperature.
2. Preheat the oven to 365 F (185° C), line the baking tray with parchment paper.
3. Beat the eggs, then mix the ingredients in a bowl to get a homogeneous "dough". Adjust amounts if needed.
4. Spread the mixture evenly on the baking tray, and bake for 30-40 minutes, until golden brown.
5. Put on a rack to cool completely.
6. Store in an airtight container or put them in the freezer to make them last longer.

Nutrition Facts:
(Analytical components in 3.5 oz)

Recipe's kcal	**203 kcal**
Fat	5.1 g
Carbohydrate	29.4 g
Fiber	2.3 g
Protein	9.1 g

WHITEFISH AND WILD RICE TREATS

Ingredients:

- 6 oz. whitefish, boiled and cooled (170 g)
- 1/2 cup cooked wild rice, cooled (85 g)
- 1/2 cup broth (125 ml)
- 2 1/2 cups all-purpose flour (250 g)
- 1/4 teaspoon salt
- 1 egg

Nutrition Facts:
(Analytical components in 3.5 oz)

Recipe's kcal	**203 kcal**
Fat	5.1 g
Carbohydrate	29.4 g
Fiber	2.3 g
Protein	9.1 g

Preparation:

1. Prepare ingredients at room temperature. Remove all the skin and fat from the thighs and breast. Remove bones if you're going to bake the loaf. Rinse meat carefully.
2. Clean liver, heart, and gizzard thoroughly, soak them in cold water, and remove connective tissues.
3. Cut thighs, breast, offal into cubes and feed them through a meat grinder.
4. Dice carrot and pumpkin into tiny cubes and add it to the mixture.
5. Mix it carefully.
6. Preheat the oven to 356 F (180° C), pour the mixture into a mold and bake for approximately 30 minutes, until golden brown.
7. Let it cool down completely, then serve or freeze in portions.

PEANUT BUTTER & BROTH DOG BISCUITS

Ingredients:

- 4.6 oz whole wheat flour (130 g)
- 4.6 oz buckwheat (cooked) (130 g)
- 2 tbsp peanut butter (Xylitol-free peanut butter) (30 g)
- 3/4 cup fish broth (200 g)
- 1/4 tsp rosehip powder (optional)

Nutrition Facts:
(Analytical components in 3.5 oz)

Recipe's kcal	**190 kcal**
Fat	5.3 g
Carbohydrate	26.2 g
Fiber	4.1 g
Protein	8.3 g

Preparation:

1. Prepare ingredients at room temperature.
2. Preheat the oven to 356 F (180° C), line the baking tray with parchment paper.
3. Mix the ingredients in a bowl or with the food blender to get a homogeneous "dough". Adjust amounts if needed.
4. Sprinkle whole wheat flour on a rolling board and roll the mixture.
5. Cut treats with knife or cookie cutters and bake for approximately 20 minutes, until golden brown. (Flip biscuits after 10 minutes.)
6. Put them on a rack to cool completely.
7. Store in an airtight container or put them in the freezer to make them last longer.

PLANT-BASED DELIGHTS

If you're all about fresh and wholesome options, this section's recipes are just right for you! These treats are fresh, healthy, light, and full of vibrant colors and flavors that your canine companion will surely relish. Packed with the natural goodness of fruits and veggies, they're a joyous celebration of taste and health.

SWEET & "SPICY" CHIPS

Ingredients:

- 7 oz sweet potato (200 g)
- 1 tsp coconut oil
- 1/4 tsp turmeric
- 1/4 tsp rosehip powder (optional)

Nutrition Facts:
(Analytical components in 3.5 oz)

Recipe's kcal	**90 kcal**	
Fat	0.1 g	
Carbohydrate	21.1 g	
Fiber	3.3 g	
Protein	2 g	

Preparation:

1. Prepare ingredients at room temperature.
2. Preheat the oven to 392 F (200° C), line the baking tray with parchment paper.
3. Peel and then dice sweet potatoes into big cubes.
4. Mix coconut oil with turmeric and rosehip powder if using, and pour onto the sweet potato.
5. Place sweet potato pieces on the baking tray
6. Bake for approximately 15 minutes, flip the pieces, and bake for another 10 minutes, until golden brown.
7. Put them on a rack to cool completely.
8. Store in an airtight container or put them in the freezer to make them last longer.

OAT & APPLE TREAT

Ingredients:

- 7 oz oat flour (or oatmeal ground to powder) (200 g)
- 1 large egg
- 3.5 oz applesauce (or pureed apple) (100 g)
- 1/4 tsp linseed oil (optional)

Nutrition Facts:
(Analytical components in 3.5 oz)

Recipe's kcal	**266 kcal**	
Fat	6.6 g	
Carbohydrate	41.3 g	
Fiber		4.4 g
Protein	10.3 g	

Preparation:

1. Prepare ingredients at room temperature.
2. Preheat the oven to 347 F (175° C), line the baking tray with parchment paper.
3. Mix the ingredients in a bowl to get a homogeneous "dough". Adjust amounts if needed.
4. Spoon the mixture into muffin tin or oven-safe silicone mold.
5. Bake for approximately 20 minutes, until golden brown.
6. Put them on a rack to cool completely.
7. Store in an airtight container or put them in the freezer to make them last longer.

SWEET POTATO & CARROT TREAT

Ingredients:

- 7 oz brown rice flour (200 g)
- 5.3 oz sweet potato (cooked, mashed) (150 g)
- 0.7 oz carrot (cooked, mashed) (20 g)
- 1 medium egg
- 1/4 tsp rosehip powder (optional)

Preparation:

1. Prepare ingredients at room temperature.
2. Preheat the oven to 347 F (175° C), line the baking tray with parchment paper.
3. Mix the ingredients in a bowl or with the food blender to get a homogeneous "dough". Adjust amounts if needed.
4. Sprinkle brown rice flour on a rolling board and roll the mixture.
5. Cut treats with knife or cookie cutters, and bake for approximately 20 minutes, until golden brown.
6. Put them on a rack to cool completely.
7. Store in an airtight container or put them in the freezer to make them last longer.

Nutrition Facts:
(Analytical components in 3.5 oz)

Recipe's kcal	**222 kcal**
Fat	2.7 g
Carbohydrate	44 g
Fiber	3.4 g
Protein	5.7 g

PUMPKIN & OATS TREAT

Ingredients:

- 7 oz oat flour (or oatmeal ground to powder) (200 g)
- 1 large egg
- 2/3 cup pumpkin puree (100 g)
- 1/4 tsp linseed oil (optional)

Preparation:

1. Prepare ingredients at room temperature.
2. Preheat the oven to 347 F (175° C), line the baking tray with parchment paper.
3. Mix the ingredients in a bowl to get a homogeneous "dough". Adjust amounts if needed.
4. Spoon the mixture into muffin tin or oven-safe silicone mold.
5. Bake for approximately 20 minutes, until golden brown.
6. Put them on a rack to cool completely.
7. Store in an airtight container or put them in the freezer to make them last longer.

Nutrition Facts:
(Analytical components in 3.5 oz)

Recipe's kcal	**257 kcal**
Fat	6.6 g
Carbohydrate	38.9 g
Fiber	4 g
Protein	10.4 g

APPLE CARROT BISCUITS

Ingredients:

- 7 oz whole-wheat flour (200 g)
- 3.5 oz rolled oats (100 g)
- 2 apples
- 2 carrots
- 1 large egg
- 1/2 tsp vegetable oil
- 1 cup water (235 ml)

Nutrition Facts:
(Analytical components in 3.5 oz)

Recipe's kcal	**255 kcal**
Fat	6.4 g
Carbohydrate	40.3 g
Fiber	8.2 g
Protein	5.3 g

Preparation:

1. Core and grate the apples. Peel and grate the carrots (using a food processor is recommended for ease).
2. In a mixing bowl, combine the dry ingredients (whole wheat flour, oats).
3. In a separate bowl, beat the egg. Mix in the vegetable oil, water, and the grated apples and carrots.
4. Add the wet ingredients to the dry ingredients. Mix thoroughly until a dough forms.
5. Roll out the dough carefully, then use a small cookie cutter to cut out the desired shapes. This recipe yields 12-24 dog biscuits, depending on your cookie cutter's size.
6. Bake the biscuits until they are firm. The exact baking time may vary based on the oven and thickness of the biscuits.

BANANA & PEANUT BUTTER TREAT

Ingredients:

- 1.4 oz oat flour (140 g)
- 1 medium, ripe banana
- 2 tbsp peanut butter (Xylitol-free peanut butter) (30 g)
- 1/4 tsp rosehip powder (optional)

Nutrition Facts:
(Analytical components in 3.5 oz)

Recipe's kcal	**312 kcal**
Fat	11.2 g
Carbohydrate	44.7 g
Fiber	5 g
Protein	10.6 g

Preparation:

1. Prepare ingredients at room temperature.
2. Preheat the oven to 338 F (170° C), line the baking tray with parchment paper.
3. Peel and then dice bananas into tiny cubes.
4. Add banana cubes and peanut butter to oat flour.
5. Mix the ingredients with the food blender to get a homogeneous "dough". Adjust amounts if needed.
6. Sprinkle oat flour on a rolling board and roll the mixture.
7. Cut treats with knife or cookie cutters and bake for approximately 20 minutes, until golden brown.
8. Put them on a rack to cool completely.
9. Store in an airtight container or put them in the freezer to make them last longer.

VEGETABLE TURMERIC DOG TREATS

Ingredients:

- 1 1/2 cups brown rice flour (300 g)
- 3/4 cup oat flour (215 g)
- 1 cup fresh baby spinach, finely chopped (30 g)
- 1 cup raw carrot, coarse grated (unpeeled) (120 g)
- 1/4 cup fresh curly parsley, chopped (16 g)
- 1/2 cup applesauce (unsweetened)
- 1/4 cup plain yogurt (low fat or fat-free) (60 g)
- 1 tsp baking powder
- 1/4 tsp turmeric powder

Optional Yogurt Glaze:

- 1/2 tsp plain yogurt
- 2 tsp water

Preparation:

1. Preheat the oven to 325°F. Line a baking tray with parchment paper or a silicone baking mat.
2. Sieve the brown rice flour and oat flour into a medium-sized bowl. Add baking powder and mix well.
3. Finely chop the spinach and parsley. Coarsely grate the carrots (leave unpeeled).
4. In a large bowl, combine spinach, parsley, carrots, and applesauce. Stir well with a wooden spoon.
5. Add yogurt to the vegetable mix. Sprinkle turmeric over the mixture and stir in thoroughly.
6. Gradually add the flour mix to the vegetable mixture, stirring well between each addition. Once all flour is incorporated, use your hands to form a dough. Knead well, adding more flour if the dough is too sticky.
7. Turn the dough out onto floured wax paper and cover with a second sheet. Roll out to 1/4" thickness. Use cookie cutters to cut into desired shapes.
8. Optional Glazing: Mix yogurt and water to form a glaze. Brush over treats before baking, if desired.
9. Bake the treats at 325°F for 35 minutes.
10. Allow the treats to cool completely. Store them in the refrigerator for 7-10 days.

Nutrition Facts:
(Analytical components in 3.5 oz)

Recipe's kcal	**266 kcal**
Fat	6.6 g
Carbohydrate	41.3 g
Fiber	4.4 g
Protein	10.3 g

NO-BAKE TREATS

If you're looking for convenience without compromising on taste, the 'No-Bake Treats' section is perfect for you and your pup! These recipes are quick, easy, and incredibly tasty, proving that great dog treats don't always require an oven. Ideal for busy pet parents, these no-fuss, no-bake delights can be whipped up in no time, offering a delicious reward for your furry friend with minimal effort.

OVERNIGHT OATS FOR DOGS

Ingredients:

- 7 oz oatmeal (200 g)
- 1 medium, ripe banana
- 2 tbsp peanut butter (Xylitol-free peanut butter) (30 g)
- 7 oz yogurt (plain, unsweetened) (200 g)

Preparation:

1. Prepare ingredients at room temperature.
2. Peel and dice banana into tiny cubes.
3. Mix the ingredients in a bowl, until fully combined. Adjust amounts if needed.
4. Pour the mixture into a container and put it in the fridge for 24 hours to let the oatmeal soak up the yogurt.
5. Before serving, let it sit for a while to reach room temperature.
6. Spoon it on top of food, or stuff it into your dog's toy.

Nutrition Facts:
(Analytical components in 3.5 oz)

- **Recipe's kcal**   **137 kcal**
- Fat   5.7 g
- Carbohydrate   13.6 g
- Fiber   1.6 g
- Protein   3.7 g

FRUIT MIX PUREE

Ingredients:

- 7 oz watermelon (diced) (200 g)
- 3.5 oz blueberries (100 g)
- 3.5 oz apple (diced) (100 g)
- 7 oz millet (cooked) (200 g)

Preparation:

1. Prepare ingredients at room temperature.
2. Put watermelon, blueberries and apple into a food blender and pulse until fully combined.
3. Add cooked millet to the mixture and pulse again to get a homogenous puree. Remove excess liquid if any. Adjust amounts if needed
4. Spoon the mixture on top of dog food or use it as an occasional treat or training snack.
5. Store in an airtight container or put it in the freezer to make it last longer.

Nutrition Facts:
(Analytical components in 3.5 oz)

- **Recipe's kcal**   **69 kcal**
- Fat   0.4 g
- Carbohydrate   15.5 g
- Fiber   1.9 g
- Protein   1.5 g

BANANA SNOWBALLS

Ingredients:

- 1 ripe banana, mashed
- 2 tbsp rosehip powder
- 1/3 cup peanut butter (Xylitol-free peanut butter) (60 g)
- 1/2 cup coconut flour (55 g)
- 1/4 cup unsweetened crisp cereal, lightly crushed (optional) (20 g)

Nutrition Facts:
(Analytical components in 3.5 oz)

Recipe's kcal	**137 kcal**	
Fat	5.7 g	
Carbohydrate	13.6 g	
Fiber	1.6 g	
Protein	3.7 g	

Preparation:

1. Mash the banana in a mixing bowl. Add the peanut butter and rosehip powder, mixing until combined.
2. Gradually add coconut flour, mixing well until the desired consistency for shaping is reached. The mixture should be slightly wet for ease of shaping and to allow coatings to stick.
3. If desired, add crushed cereal for extra crunch. (Optional)
4. Roll the mixture into small, bite-sized balls.
5. Coat in additional desiccated coconut or leave plain. (Optional)
6. Refrigerate the treats until firm.
7. Store in the fridge for short-term or freeze for longer storage.

EASY PUMPKIN & CINNAMON TREATS

Ingredients:

- 1 cup coconut oil (235 ml)
- 3/4 cup canned pumpkin (170 g)
- 1/2 cup peanut butter (125 g) (Xylitol-free peanut butter)
- 1 tsp cinnamon
- 1 tsp maple syrup
- 1 1/2 tbsp flaxseed (optional)

Nutrition Facts:
(Analytical components in 3.5 oz)

Recipe's kcal	**110 kcal**	
Fat	1.4 g	
Carbohydrate	9.5 g	
Fiber	3.9 g	
Protein	2.5 g	

Preparation:

1. Place silicone molds on a counter, plate, or baking sheet for stability.
2. In a large saucepan over medium-low heat, combine all ingredients. Stir occasionally until the coconut oil melts and the mixture is well incorporated.
3. Remove the saucepan from heat and let the mixture cool for about 1 minute.
4. Pour the mixture into the molds. For easier filling, consider using a piping bag, though this step is optional.
5. Place the molds in the freezer for about 1 hour, or until the treats are set.
6. Remove the treats from the molds and store them in an airtight container in the refrigerator or freezer. They should last about 7 days in the refrigerator.

DOG PUMPKIN-BALLS

Ingredients:

- 1 cup pumpkin puree (225 g)
- 1/2 cup peanut butter (115 g) (Xylitol-free peanut butter)
- 2 1/2 cups oats rolled (335 g)
- 1/4 cup honey (56 g)
- 1 tsp cinnamon

Preparation:

1. In a large bowl, thoroughly mix the oats, peanut butter, pumpkin puree, honey, and cinnamon until fully combined.
2. Form the mixture into 1 1/2" balls and place them on a parchment-lined baking sheet.
3. Chill the balls for 1 hour in the refrigerator, then transfer them to an airtight container for storage.

Nutrition Facts:
(Analytical components in 3.5 oz)

- **Recipe's kcal   124 kcal**
- Fat   5 g
- Carbohydrate   16 g
- Fiber   2 g
- Protein   4.5 g

BACON & BANANA SNOWBALLS

Ingredients:

- 3 slices cooked bacon
- 2 ripe bananas
- 1 tbls coconut oil
- 1 cup old fashioned rolled oats uncooked (80 g)
- 1/2 cup peanut butter (125 g) (Xylitol-free peanut butter)
- 1/2 cup unsweetened coconut flakes (50 g)

Preparation:

1. If the bacon isn't already cooked, cook it until crispy. Then, chop the cooked bacon into small pieces.
2. Place the bananas in a medium mixing bowl and mash them with a fork.
3. In the bowl with the mashed bananas, add the rolled oats, melted coconut oil, peanut butter, chopped bacon, and coconut flakes.
4. Blend the mixture well using a hand mixer, spoon, or your hands.
5. The dough will be sticky. Let it sit in the refrigerator for 30 minutes to stiffen up.
6. Roll the dough into balls about 1 to 1½ inches thick and place them on a tray.
7. Refrigerate the tray until the treats harden to the touch, approximately 30 minutes to 1 hour.

Nutrition Facts:
(Analytical components in 3.5 oz)

- **Recipe's kcal   120 kcal**
- Fat   9 g
- Carbohydrate   10 g
- Fiber   2 g
- Protein   4.5 g

OVERNIGHT OATS & FRUITS FOR DOGS

Ingredients:

- 7 oz oatmeal (200 g)
- 1/2 medium apple, peeled and finely diced (100 g)
- 1/4 cup blueberries (fresh or frozen) (40 gr)
- 1/4 cup pumpkin puree (plain, unsweetened) (60 g)
- 7 oz yogurt (plain, unsweetened) (200 g)

Nutrition Facts:
(Analytical components in 3.5 oz)

Recipe's kcal	**137 kcal**	
Fat	5.7 g	
Carbohydrate	13.6 g	
Fiber	1.6 g	
Protein	3.7 g	

Preparation:

1. Prepare Ingredients: Ensure all ingredients are at room temperature.
2. Dice Apple: Peel and finely dice the apple into small pieces. Ensure there are no seeds.
3. Prepare Blueberries: If using frozen blueberries, thaw them beforehand. For fresh blueberries, wash them thoroughly.
4. Mix Ingredients: In a bowl, combine the oatmeal, diced apple, blueberries, pumpkin puree, and yogurt. Stir until well blended.
5. Refrigerate: Transfer the mixture into a container and place it in the fridge for 24 hours. This allows the oats to absorb the flavors and soften.
6. Serving: Before serving, let the mixture come to room temperature. It can be served alone as a special treat or spooned over your dog's regular food.

2-INGREDIENTS RECIPES

Let's celebrate the simplicity of using just two ingredients, while they come together to create something truly special for your furry friend. These easy-to-make, nutritious treats are perfect if you want to give your friend homemade goodness without the hassle. Despite their simplicity, these treats are a fantastic option that provides both flavor and nutrition for your dog. Remember, moderation is key, even with these simple and wholesome treats.

BANANA BITES

Ingredients:

- 2 ripe bananas
- 1 cup rolled oats (90 g)

Nutrition Facts:
(Analytical components in 3.5 oz)

- **Recipe's kcal   98 kcal**
- Fat   6 g
- Carbohydrate   10 g
- Fiber   7 g
- Protein   2 g

Preparation:

1. Preheat your oven to 350°F (175°C). Line a baking sheet with parchment paper.
2. In a bowl, mash the ripe bananas until smooth.
3. Mix the oats into the mashed bananas until well combined.
4. Scoop small spoonfuls of the banana-oat mixture onto the prepared baking sheet.
5. Gently flatten each spoonful with the back of a spoon to form bite-sized treats.
6. Bake the banana bites for about 12-15 minutes, or until the edges turn golden brown.
7. Allow the treats to cool completely before serving to your dog.

Storage and Tips:

- Store any leftovers for a few days in an airtight container for optimal freshness.
- Bananas are a good source of potassium, vitamins, and fiber.
- Oats provide dietary fiber and are gentle on a dog's digestive system.

BACON & PEAR

Ingredients:

- 3 large pears
- 10.6 oz bacon (sliced) (300 g)

Preparation:

1. Core pear and cut into thin slices.
2. Wrap pear slices with bacon.
3. Place wrapped slices on a baking tray lined with parchment paper.
4. Set the oven to the lowest temperature and bake until crispy.
   For best results, use a food dehydrator.

Nutrition Facts:
(Analytical components in 3.5 oz)

- **Recipe's kcal   196 kcal**
- Fat   12.1 g
- Carbohydrate   10.1 g
- Fiber   1.9 g
- Protein   12.2 g

PAWNUT BUTTER FREEZE TREATS

Ingredients:

- 1 cup peanut butter (Xylitol-free peanut butter) (250 g)
- 1 tsp unprocessed coconut oil
- Silicon paw print tray (or any silicon mold)

Nutrition Facts:
(Analytical components in 3.5 oz)

- **Recipe's kcal** **101 kcal**
- Fat   2.6 g
- Carbohydrate   19.2 g
- Fiber   2.1 g
- Protein   2.9 g

Preparation:

1. Ensure the coconut oil is in liquid form. If it's solid, melt it by placing the coconut oil in a small saucepan over medium-low heat until it becomes liquid.
2. Add the peanut butter to the melted coconut oil. Stir the mixture until it becomes completely smooth and thoroughly mixed. The mixture should be thick but pourable.
3. Pour the peanut butter and coconut oil mixture into the silicon paw print tray or your chosen mold.
4. Place the tray in the freezer and leave it until the treats are set and firm.
5. Carefully pop the treats out of the tray. Store them in an airtight container in the freezer, as they tend to soften quickly at room temperature.

Storage and Tips:

- Serve these treats as a frozen snack, particularly refreshing during warmer weather.
- Peanut butter provides protein and healthy fats, but ensure it's xylitol-free and unsweetened for dog safety.
- Coconut oil can aid in creating a healthy coat and skin.

PUMPKIN & BANANA

Ingredients:

- 3 medium, ripe bananas
- 3.5 oz pumpkin (baked, pureed, unsweetened) (100 g)

Preparation:

1. Puree banana and pumpkin, and mix well until fully combined.
2. Scoop mixture into ice trays or freezer-safe silicone mold and freeze.

Nutrition Facts:
(Analytical components in 3.5 oz)

- **Recipe's kcal** **70 kcal**
- Fat   0.2 g
- Carbohydrate   18 g
- Fiber   2.2 g
- Protein   1 g

SARDINE DOG BISCUITS

Ingredients:

- 1 standard-sized tinned sardines, drained, reserve the drained liquid
- 2/3 cup oatmeal or other flour (plus extra for rolling out) (55 g)

Nutrition Facts:
(Analytical components in 3.5 oz)

- **Recipe's kcal**   **173 kcal**
- Fat   8.9 g
- Carbohydrate   7.1 g
- Fiber   0.9 g
- Protein   15.8 g

Preparation:

1. Preheat the oven to 350°F (approx 177°C).
2. Cut a piece of baking or greaseproof paper to fit a baking tray of approximately 12 x 8 inches.
3. Drain the sardines, reserving the liquid. Mash the sardines roughly with a fork in a bowl.
4. Add the oatmeal or chosen flour to the sardines. Mix in 1 tablespoon of the reserved liquid to form a dough, adding more liquid as needed but avoiding making the dough too wet.
5. Knead the dough briefly on a surface dusted with oatmeal or flour.
6. Place the dough on the prepared baking paper on a work surface. Dust the dough and a rolling pin with extra oatmeal or flour, then roll out to a thin rectangle (about 1/16 to 1/8 inch thick).
7. Cut the dough into squares or rectangles using a knife or pizza wheel. Neaten the edges first, and re-roll the scraps to cut more biscuits with a cookie cutter if desired.
8. Transfer the baking paper with biscuits onto a tray. Bake on the middle shelf of the oven until dry and cooked through (40-50 minutes). Turn biscuits over halfway through for even cooking. Remove edge biscuits earlier if they cook faster.
9. Cool the biscuits completely on a wire rack, then store in an airtight container. They should stay fresh for at least 2 weeks. They can also be frozen and fed without defrosting if rolled thinly.

Storage and Tips:

- Preferably use sardines in spring water. Alternative tinned fish like pilchards, tuna, mackerel, or salmon can be used.
- Flour Alternatives: Use any flour or combination of flours. Wheat-free alternatives include rice flour or gram (chickpea) flour. For grain-free or gluten-free options, coconut flour is suitable. Flour types absorb different amounts of liquid, so adjust accordingly. Use plain water, low salt stock, milk, or yogurt if additional liquid is needed.
- Sardines are rich in omega-3 fatty acids and protein.

EASY SWEET POTATOES BISCUITS

Ingredients:

- 2 cups whole wheat flour (240 g)
- 8 oz sweet Potato puree (225 g)

Nutrition Facts:
(Analytical components in 3.5 oz)

Recipe's kcal	**101 kcal**
Fat	1.6 g
Carbohydrate	15.2 g
Fiber	5.1 g
Protein	2.9 g

Preparation:

1. Preheat the oven to 350° F (175° C). Coat a baking sheet with non-stick cooking spray, or alternatively, line it with a silicone baking mat or parchment paper.
2. In a large bowl, whisk together the whole wheat flour and sweet potato puree. If the mixture is too thick and difficult to stir, you can add up to a tablespoon of water to achieve the right consistency.
3. On a floured surface, roll out the dough using a rolling pin to about 1/2" thickness, similar to making cookies.
4. Use a cookie cutter to cut out the biscuits from the rolled dough.
5. Place the biscuits on the prepared baking sheet, ensuring a little space between each one. Bake for 20-25 minutes until they turn golden brown and there is no visible moisture. Be careful not to burn them.
6. Allow the biscuits to cool down before serving them to your dog.

Storage and Tips:

- Whole wheat flour provides dietary fiber and is a healthy carbohydrate source.
- Sweet potato is rich in vitamins, minerals, and fiber, making it a nutritious choice for dogs.

FROZEN TREATS & JELLY

Dive into the refreshing world of 'Frozen Treats & Jelly', where we've crafted an array of frosty delights perfect for those hot summer days or as cool rewards during training sessions. Made with fruit and their natural sugars, these treats are a delightful way to pamper your dog while being mindful of their health. Remember, as tempting and refreshing as they might be for your pet, it's important to serve these frozen goodies in moderation to maintain a balanced diet.

FROZEN BANANA

Ingredients:

- 3 medium, ripe bananas

Preparation:

1. Cut the banana into cubes and freeze in an ice tray or freezer-safe silicone mold. This is the ultimate quick treat on hot summer days. It's as simple as that!

Nutrition Facts:
(Analytical components in 3.5 oz)

- **Recipe's kcal**   **89 kcal**
- Fat   0.3 g
- Carbohydrate   23 g
- Fiber   2.6 g
- Protein   1.1 g

PEANUT BUTTER & BANANA

Ingredients:

- 3 medium, ripe bananas
- 2 tbsp peanut butter (Xylitol-free peanut butter) (30 g)
- 3.5 oz yogurt (unsweetened, unflavored) (100 g)

Preparation:

1. Puree banana, then mix ingredients in a bowl.
2. Scoop mixture into ice trays or freezer-safe silicone mold and freeze.

Storage and Tips:

- Serve these frozen treats as a refreshing and healthy snack for your dog, especially on warm days.
- Bananas are a good source of potassium, vitamins, and fiber.

Nutrition Facts:
(Analytical components in 3.5 oz)

- **Recipe's kcal**   **101 kcal**
- Fat   2.6 g
- Carbohydrate   19.2 g
- Fiber   2.1 g
- Protein   2.9 g

FROZEN HEN SOUP

Ingredients:

- 2 3/4 cup water (650 g)
- 5.3 oz chicken thighs (150 g)
- 3.5 oz carrot (100 g)
- 1.7 oz pumpkin (baked) (50 g)
- 1.7 oz apple (50 g)
- 1 tsp rosehip powder (optional)

Nutrition Facts:
(Analytical components in 3.5 oz)

- **Recipe's kcal**   **41 kcal**
- Fat   2.1 g
- Carbohydrate   2 g
- Fiber   0.5 g
- Protein   3.8 g

Preparation:

1. Prepare ingredients at room temperature. Rinse meat carefully. Remove bones from the thighs, leave skin and fat on.
2. Clean thighs carefully if necessary.
3. Cut meat into cubes.
4. Cook meat in water for approximately 15 minutes (amount of water depends on personal preferences) slowly to preserve nutrients.
5. Peel and cut baked pumpkin and carrot into tiny cubes.
6. Add carrot, apple, and pumpkin to the mixture, incorporating it carefully.
7. Pour the mixture into a food processor and mix it to get a homogeneous liquid. You can use a stick blender for mixing.
8. Let the mixture cool down, add rosehip powder, then pour into an ice tray or silicone molds and freeze. Perfect training snack on hot summer days!

BERRY ICE CREAM

Ingredients:

- 7 oz yogurt (200 g)
- 3.5 oz beetroot (cooked) (100 g)
- 0.7 oz banana (20 g)
- 0.7 oz blueberries (20 g)

Preparation:

1. Puree beetroot, blueberries, and banana.
2. Add yogurt to the mixture and mix until fully combined.
3. Scoop mixture into ice tray or popsicle mold and freeze.

Nutrition Facts:
(Analytical components in 3.5 oz)

- **Recipe's kcal**   **57 kcal**
- Fat   3.2 g
- Carbohydrate   9.3 g
- Fiber   0.9 g
- Protein   3.6 g

DOG GUMMIES

Ingredients:

- 2 tbsp plain, unflavored gelatin
- 3/4 cup broth (liver, chicken, or beef) (180 ml)
- 1 tbsp olive oil (for greasing)
- ice trays or silicone trays

Nutrition Facts:
(Analytical components in 3.5 oz)

Recipe's kcal	**57 kcal**	
Fat	3.2 g	
Carbohydrate	9.3 g	
Fiber	0.9 g	
Protein	3.6 g	

Preparation:

1. Lightly grease the ice cube trays or silicone molds with olive oil using a mister or by brushing each mold.
2. Sprinkle 2 tablespoons (equivalent to 2 packets) of unflavored gelatin over 1/4 cup of cold broth. Allow it to bloom for a minute.
3. Warm another 1/2 cup of broth in a saucepan or microwave until it boils.
4. Combining Broth and Gelatin: Pour the hot broth into the cold broth and gelatin mixture. Stir until completely mixed.
5. Pour the mixture into the prepared trays. If using floppy silicone trays, place them on a cookie sheet before filling for easy movement.
6. Refrigerate the gummies for 4-5 hours until set.
7. Pop the gummies out of the trays.

Storage and Tips:

- Try different broth bases like chicken, beef, or bone broth (homemade to avoid onion powder).
- For added nutrients, mix in pulverized blueberries, green beans, turmeric, spirulina, small pieces of banana…
- Be creative with the shapes and sizes, especially if using them as pill pockets.

CANTALOUPE ICE CREAM

Ingredients:

- 2 cups frozen ripe cantaloupe (300 g)
- 2 tbsp unsweetened yogurt

Nutrition Facts:
(Analytical components in 3.5 oz)

Recipe's kcal	**59 kcal**	
Fat	4.2 g	
Carbohydrate	7.3 g	
Fiber	1.9 g	
Protein	2.6 g	

Preparation:

1. Ensure there is enough space in your freezer for the cantaloupe.
2. Scrub the outside of the cantaloupe thoroughly to clean it.
3. Cut the cantaloupe in half and remove the seeds. Slice each half into quarters, remove the rind, and dice the fruit into bite-sized chunks.
4. Place the diced cantaloupe in the freezer. For quicker freezing, spread the pieces on a baking sheet to allow more space around each chunk.
5. Allow the cantaloupe to freeze completely, which can take 2-4 hours or can be left overnight.
6. Once frozen, put about 2 cups (300g) of frozen cantaloupe pieces into the food processor. Add 2 tablespoons of unsweetened yogurt.
7. Blend the mixture until combined, adding a little cool water if necessary to achieve your preferred consistency.

Storage and Tips:

- Freeze the mixture into paw-shaped molds for homemade frozen dog treats.
- Cantaloupe is a good source of vitamins and hydration.
- Unsweetened yogurt provides calcium and probiotics.

FROZEN PUMPKIN DELIGHT

Ingredients:

- 1/2 cup greek yogurt (130 g)
- 1/2 cup pumpkin puree (115 g)

Preparation:

1. In a medium bowl, combine the Greek yogurt and pumpkin puree. Stir until well mixed.
2. Use a small spoon to carefully fill the silicone molds with the mixture.
3. Place the molds in the freezer and allow the mixture to chill and set for about 3 hours.
4. Once frozen, unmold the treats and store them in an airtight container in the freezer.

Nutrition Facts:
(Analytical components in 3.5 oz)

- **Recipe's kcal** **59 kcal**
- Fat   4.2 g
- Carbohydrate 7.3 g
- Fiber   1.9 g
- Protein   2.6 g

TRAINING TREATS

If training sessions are a regular part of your day, you're going to love these recipes! Creating these protein-rich, bite-sized treats is easier than you might imagine. They're perfect for use during training, being small enough to be convenient yet packed with protein to keep your dog energized. Plus, you'll find snacks ideal for after training too, perfect as a reward for a job well done and for providing a quick energy boost.

BEEF AFTER TRAINING SNACK

Ingredients:

- 1.75 oz ground beef (50 g)
- 1 egg yolk
- 20 blueberries
- 1.75 oz rolled oats (50 g)

Nutrition Facts:
(Analytical components in 3.5 oz)

	Recipe's kcal	302 kcal
•	Fat	11.2 g
•	Carbohydrate	7.1 g
•	Fiber	0.9 g
•	Protein	18 g

Preparation:

1. Chop the rolled oats into smaller pieces.
2. In a non-stick skillet, lightly cook the ground beef with a little water until it's fully cooked. Be sure not to use any oil or seasoning.
3. In a small pot, stew the blueberries over low heat with just enough water to barely cover them.
4. Allow the cooked beef to cool. Meanwhile, blend the stewed blueberries into a puree.
5. In a bowl, combine the cooked beef, chopped oats, and egg yolk. Mix well.
6. Stir in the blueberry puree.
7. Serve the mixture once it's cooled down to a safe temperature.

Storage and Tips:

- Serve this as a special treat after a long training session
- Ground beef provides protein and essential nutrients, Egg yolk is rich in vitamins and healthy fats.

EASY TRAINING TREATS

Ingredients:

- 2 cups oat flour or ground oats (160 g)
- 1/2 cup peanut butter (Xylitol-free peanut butter) (112 g)
- 1/4 cup applesauce (no sugar added) (60 ml)
- 1/4 cup chicken or beef broth (60 ml)

Nutrition Facts:
(Analytical components in 3.5 oz)

	Recipe's kcal	182 kcal
•	Fat	7.2 g
•	Carbohydrate	7.1 g
•	Fiber	1.9 g
•	Protein	9 g

Preparation:

1. Preheat the oven to 350°F (180°C).
2. In a medium mixing bowl, add the oat flour (or ground oats), peanut butter, applesauce, and broth.
3. Using a sturdy rubber spatula or spoon, stir the mixture until it becomes uniform. The dough will be stiff, so you'll need a strong tool for mixing.
4. Roll the dough out into a rough rectangle. Rolling it between sheets of parchment paper can help avoid sticking and the need for extra flour.
5. Cut the dough into one-inch squares (similar in size to a Cheez-It cracker). Using a pizza cutter can make this process quicker and easier than using a knife.
6. Combine any edge pieces and reshape them into one-inch squares to avoid waste.
7. Space the treats out on one of the parchment papers used for rolling. Place the parchment on a baking sheet and bake for 14-16 minutes.
8. Allow the treats to cool completely before feeding them to your dog.
9. Store the treats in an airtight container in the refrigerator.

LIGHT AFTER TRAINING SNACK

Ingredients:

- 2.5 oz greek yogurt (70 g)
- 1 tsp honey
- 6 pumpkin seeds
- 1 tsp salmon oil

Preparation:

1. Shell the pumpkin seeds, if necessary. Toast them in a non-stick skillet without any salt. Allow them to cool after toasting.
2. Once cooled, grind the toasted pumpkin seeds into a fine powder.
3. In a bowl, combine the greek yogurt, honey, and salmon oil. Stir them together well.
4. Mix in the ground pumpkin seeds.

Storage and Tips:

- Store any leftovers in the refrigerator and use within a few days for freshness.
- Ricotta is a good source of calcium and protein. Honey provides natural sweetness and contains small amounts of vitamins and minerals.
- Salmon oil is a great source of omega-3 fatty acids, beneficial for a dog's coat and skin health.

Nutrition Facts:
(Analytical components in 3.5 oz)

- **Recipe's kcal**   **222 kcal**
- Fat   9.2 g
- Carbohydrate   7.1 g
- Fiber   4.9 g
- Protein   8 g

BANANA AFTER TRAINING SNACK

Ingredients:

- 1 ripe banana
- 1 tsp honey
- 2 rice cakes
- 1 tbsp peanut butter (Xylitol-free peanut butter) (15 g)

Preparation:

1. Grind the rice cakes into a fine powder.
2. In a bowl, mash the ripe banana. Mix in half of the ground rice cakes and the honey.
3. Add the remaining half of the ground rice cakes and the peanut butter to the mixture. Combine well until you have a compact mixture.
4. Divide the mixture into flattened patties or discs, sized appropriately for your dog's mouth. They should be chewable, not small enough to be swallowed whole.

Storage and Tips:

- Store any leftovers in the refrigerator and use within a few days for freshness.
- Rice cakes offer a low-fat, crunchy texture, your dog will love it
- Peanut butter is a source of protein and healthy fats

Nutrition Facts:
(Analytical components in 3.5 oz)

- **Recipe's kcal**   **211 kcal**
- Fat   7.2 g
- Carbohydrate   9.1 g
- Fiber   4.4 g
- Protein   3 g

SALMON SWIRL TRAINING TREATS

Ingredients:

- 1 can of salmon (include the juices)
- 2 cups rolled oats (300 g)
- 2 large eggs
- 1 tbsp fish oil (optional)

Nutrition Facts:
(Analytical components in 3.5 oz)

- **Recipe's kcal** **201 kcal**
- Fat   5.1 g
- Carbohydrate   27.9 g
- Fiber   1.9 g
- Protein   9.1 g

Preparation:

1. Preheat the oven to 350°F (177°C), positioning both racks near the center but accessible.
2. Place rolled oats in the food processor and pulse for about a minute to create oat flour.
3. Add the entire can of salmon, including the juices, to the oat flour in the food processor.
4. Pulse to combine well. Add the eggs and continue pulsing until a dough ball forms.
5. Check the consistency of your dough. It should be easy to pipe but firm enough to hold the swirl shape. If necessary, adjust by adding water or a little more flour (or cornstarch). Alternatively, you can briefly set the dough in the freezer.
6. Pipe the dough onto the parchment-covered cookie sheets using the pastry bag with an open swirl tip.
7. Bake the treats until they show a bit of color on the bottom and edges, aiming for a dry and crunchy texture. The total baking time should be about 30 minutes. Rotate and swap the pans halfway through. If necessary, continue baking and check every five minutes until done.
8. Allow the treats to cool completely before serving or storing.

MICROWAVED HOT DOG TRAINING TREATS

Ingredients:

- 1 package hot dogs (preferably turkey or beef, and organic if possible)

Nutrition Facts:
(Analytical components in 3.5 oz)

- **Recipe's kcal** **121 kcal**
- Fat   5.1 g
- Carbohydrate   7.9 g
- Fiber   0.9 g
- Protein   11.1 g

Preparation:

1. Cut the hot dogs into small slices, about 1/4 inch thick. For training purposes, you can optionally divide each slice into two or four smaller pieces.
2. Place the hot dog slices on a stack of six paper towels.
3. Cover the slices with another paper towel.
4. Microwave the hot dog slices for 3-5 minutes, depending on your microwave's strength.
5. Uncover and stir the hot dog slices to ensure they are cooking evenly. If needed, microwave for an additional 3 minutes.
6. Once done, remove the slices from the microwave and blot all excess oil with paper towels.
7. Allow the hot dog slices to cool completely before serving.
8. Refrigerate the treats for up to a week or freeze them for longer storage.

TUNA SOFT TREATS FOR TRAINING

Ingredients:

- 1 tin (about 5.3-5.6 oz) tuna in oil (150 g)
- 1 large egg
- 3/4 cup wholemeal, white wheat flour, or rice flour (95 g)
- 1/2 cup water (100 ml)

Nutrition Facts:
(Analytical components in 3.5 oz)

- **Recipe's kcal** **127 kcal**
- Fat 5.1 g
- Carbohydrate 9.7 g
- Fiber 0.9 g
- Protein 9.3 g

Preparation:

1. Put the entire contents of the tuna tin, including the oil, into a blender. Add the egg, flour, and water.
2. Blend until you have a thick, smooth batter.
3. Pour the batter into a microwave-safe container approximately 5 x 3 inches and smooth the top. Adjust cooking time if using a different size container.
4. Microwave on high power for 1 minute. Remove and prick all over with a skewer to remove air pockets.
5. Return to the microwave and cook for a further 3 minutes. Tip out onto a board, then slide back into the container so that the bottom is now on top. Microwave for another 4 minutes.
6. Transfer to a board to cool; placing the kitchen towel underneath will absorb excess steam.
7. When completely cold, cut into bite-sized pieces. For slightly crunchy treats, microwave the pieces for another 4-5 minutes.
8. Store in an airtight container in the fridge for up to a week. Can also be frozen and defrosted as needed.

Storage and Tips:

- Grain-Free Alternative: For grain-free options, try gram (chickpea) or coconut flour. Adjust by adding extra liquid to achieve a thick batter.
- These tuna treats are perfect for training sessions due to their size and flavor.

SMALL BITE-SIZED REWARDS

Ingredients:

- 3 jars of chicken baby food
- 1/4 cup cream of wheat (about 2 packets) (135 g)
- 1/2 cup broth (120 g)

Nutrition Facts:
(Analytical components in 3.5 oz)

- **Recipe's kcal** **135 kcal**
- Fat 4.1 g
- Carbohydrate 5.9 g
- Fiber 2.9 g
- Protein 15.1 g

Preparation:

1. Preheat the oven to 350 degrees F (175 degrees C).
2. In a bowl, combine the chicken baby food, Cream of Wheat, and broth. Mix well until the batter is uniform.
3. Pour the batter onto the backside of a pyramid baking mat (or a similar non-stick baking mat). Use a spatula to spread the batter evenly.
4. Bake the treats for about 20-30 minutes, or until they turn brown.
5. Allow the treats to cool on wire racks.

Storage and Tips:

- The use of baby food makes these treats suitable for dogs with sensitive stomachs or those who prefer softer textures and do not contain any ingredients that are harmful to dogs.
- Serve these bite-sized treats as rewards during training sessions or as a special snack.
- Refrigerate them for up to four days, or freeze them for longer storage.

LOW-CALORIES TREATS

If you're mindful about not overfeeding your pup but still want to offer them something delicious, these recipes are exactly what you need! They are designed for weight control, ensuring your dog can enjoy tasty snacks without the worry of excess calories. So flavorful, even the pickiest of eaters will find them irresistible. With these treats, you can satisfy your furry friend's cravings while keeping their health and weight in check.

ZUCCHINI LIGHT CHIPS

Ingredients:

- 1 medium zucchini
- 1/3 cup rice flour (50 g)
- A pinch of thyme

Preparation:

1. Preheat the oven to 355°F (180°C).
2. Wash the zucchini, trim the ends, and slice it thinly.
3. Lightly spritz the zucchini slices with water, then season with a pinch of thyme or mixed herbs.
4. Lightly coat the seasoned zucchini slices with rice flour.
5. Line a shallow baking tray with parchment paper and arrange the zucchini slices on it.
6. Bake the zucchini chips for 15 minutes. Keep an eye on them to prevent burning. If they don't seem crispy enough, bake for an additional 5 minutes.
7. Allow the chips to cool down completely before offering them to your dog.

Nutrition Facts:
(Analytical components in 3.5 oz)

- **Recipe's kcal**   **49 kcal**
- Fat   0.1 g
- Carbohydrate   0.9 g
- Fiber   4.9 g
- Protein   1.1 g

BOILED EGG DOG TREAT

Ingredients:

- 1 egg

Preparation:

1. Place the egg in a pot of boiling water. Boil until the egg is hard-boiled, which usually takes about 10-12 minutes.
2. Carefully remove the egg with a slotted spoon and let it cool down.
3. Once cooled, peel the egg. Cut it in half. Store one half in the refrigerator for the next day.
4. Offer half of the boiled egg to your dog as is, or cut it into smaller pieces for easier consumption.

Nutrition Facts:
(Analytical components in 3.5 oz)

- **Recipe's kcal**   **155 kcal**
- Fat   11 g
- Carbohydrate   1.1 g
- Fiber   0 g
- Protein   13 g

LIGHT SHRIMP, SALMON OIL, AND APPLE DOG TREAT

Ingredients:

- 6 shrimp
- 1 apple
- 1 tsp salmon oil (2-3 g)

Nutrition Facts:
(Analytical components in 3.5 oz)

- **Recipe's kcal**   **90 kcal**
- Fat   8 g
- Carbohydrate   1.1 g
- Fiber   3 g
- Protein   18 g

Preparation:

1. Boil the shrimp and let them cool. Once cooled, peel the shrimp.
2. Peel the apple, remove the core and seeds, and cut it into small pieces. Place the apple pieces in a small pot.
3. Add just enough water to barely cover the apple pieces. Cook over low heat until the apple is soft.
4. Once the apple is cooked and cooled, blend it into a puree. Add a teaspoon of salmon oil to the apple puree and mix well.
5. Cut the cooked shrimp into pieces that are appropriately sized for your dog's mouth.
6. In your dog's bowl, pour the apple sauce, and then place the shrimp pieces on top. Serve this delightful treat to your furry friend.

EASY LOW-FAT BISCUITS

Ingredients:

- 1/4 cup of pumpkin puree (60 g)
- 2 eggs
- 1/4 cup water (60 ml)
- 3 tbsp peanut butter (Xylitol-free peanut butter)
- 1/2 tsp salt (optional)
- 1/2 tsp cinnamon (optional)
- 3 cups whole-wheat flour or rice flour (360 g)

Nutrition Facts:
(Analytical components in 3.5 oz)

- **Recipe's kcal**   **125 kcal**
- Fat   19 g
- Carbohydrate   3.1 g
- Fiber   7 g
- Protein   18 g

Preparation:

1. Preheat your oven to 350°F on convection setting or 375°F on conventional.
2. In a stand mixer with a dough hook (or by hand), combine the pumpkin puree, eggs, water, peanut butter, salt, and cinnamon. Gradually mix in the flour until the consistency is similar to pie dough. You may need to add more water to achieve the right texture.
3. If mixing by hand, start in the bowl and then move to a floured surface to finish combining.
4. Place the dough on a lightly floured surface and cut it in half for easier handling. Roll out each half to about 1/4 inch thick.
5. Use bone-shaped or other cookie cutters to cut out the treats. Alternatively, roll the dough into logs of 1-inch diameter and cut into 1/4 to 1/2 inch pieces.
6. Prepare two large baking sheets with parchment paper and distribute the biscuits evenly.
7. Bake for 30 minutes for semi-hard treats or longer for harder ones. Ensure the treats reach an internal temperature of 165°F for food safety due to the eggs.

Storage and Tips:

- For a lower fat version, use 4 egg whites instead of 2 whole eggs or 4 egg whites

LOW-CALORIE BROTH DOGGY TREATS

Ingredients:

- 2 cups oat flour or ground oats (160 g)
- 1/2 cup shredded carrots (70 g)
- 1/2 cup ground flaxseed (30 g)
- 1/4 cup applesauce (no sugar added) (60 ml)
- 1 egg white
- 1/4 cup chicken or bone broth (60 ml)

Nutrition Facts:
(Analytical components in 3.5 oz)

- **Recipe's kcal**   **105 kcal**
- Fat   13 g
- Carbohydrate   4.1 g
- Fiber   8 g
- Protein   9 g

Preparation:

1. Preheat the oven to 350°F.
2. In a large bowl, mix together the oat flour, flaxseed, and shredded carrots.
3. Add the bone broth, applesauce, and egg white to the dry ingredients.
4. Stir until the ingredients are well combined and a dough forms.
5. Roll out the dough using a rolling pin.
6. Place the dough on parchment paper on a cookie sheet (or roll it out on parchment for easier transfer). Cut the dough into 1-inch squares using a pizza cutter or knife.
7. Bake the treats for about 15 minutes, or until they are golden brown.
8. Let the treats cool on the baking sheet before breaking them apart.
9. Store the treats in an airtight container at room temperature.

TUNA & TURMERIC DOG TREAT

Ingredients:

- 1 cup oat flour (125 g)
- 1/2 cup buckwheat flour (65 g)
- 1/2 cup of tuna (5 oz can, either in oil or water) (115 g)
- 1/3 cup nutritional yeast (40 g)
- 1/3 cup fresh curly parsley, finely chopped (20 g)
- 1/4 cup water (60 ml)
- 1 tbsp olive oil
- 1 1/2 tsp turmeric

Nutrition Facts:
(Analytical components in 3.5 oz)

- **Recipe's kcal**   **115 kcal**
- Fat   12 g
- Carbohydrate   4.1 g
- Fiber   9 g
- Protein   14 g

Preparation:

1. Preheat the oven to 350°F.
2. Line a baking tray with a silicone baking mat.
3. Finely chop the parsley using a sharp knife.
4. Mash the tuna in a small bowl.
5. In a large bowl, stir together the oat flour and buckwheat flour with the nutritional yeast.
6. Mix the olive oil into the mashed tuna.
7. Add the tuna mixture and chopped parsley to the dry ingredients. Mix well. Gradually add water and use your hands to form the dough.
8. Turn the dough out onto lightly floured wax paper. Use a lightly floured rolling pin to roll the dough to approximately 1/4 inch thickness.
9. Cut out treats using a cookie cutter or sharp knife.
10. Bake the treats at 350°F for about 15 minutes or until they are golden and firm to the touch.
11. Remove the treats from the oven and allow them to cool completely.
12. Store the treats in an airtight container in the refrigerator for up to one week.

LIGHT PUMPKIN & BANANA TREATS

Ingredients:

- 2 cups whole-wheat flour (250 g)
- 1 ripe banana, mashed
- 1 cup pumpkin puree (225 g)
- 1 tbsp barley malt syrup
- 1 tbsp ground flaxseed

Nutrition Facts:
(Analytical components in 3.5 oz)

- **Recipe's kcal**   **111 kcal**
- Fat   9 g
- Carbohydrate   3.1 g
- Fiber   17 g
- Protein   9 g

Preparation:

1. Preheat the oven to 350°F.
2. Line a baking tray with parchment paper or a silicone baking mat.
3. Mash the banana in a bowl.
4. In a large bowl, combine the mashed banana, pumpkin puree, and barley malt syrup. Use a fork to mix these ingredients together well.
5. In a separate bowl, mix the ground flaxseed with the whole-wheat flour.
6. Gradually add the dry ingredients to the wet mixture, one cup at a time, and combine well using a wooden spoon. The dough should be dry; if it's too sticky, add a bit more flour until you achieve the right consistency.
7. Roll out the dough and cut into desired shapes. Place on the prepared baking tray.
8. Bake in the preheated oven until the treats are golden and firm. The baking time will vary based on the size and thickness of the treats.

LOW CALORIE PUMPKIN & SPINACH TREATS

Ingredients:

- 1 cup whole-wheat flour (125 g)
- 1/2 cup pumpkin puree (115 g)
- 1/2 cup fresh baby spinach, finely chopped (40 g)
- 1 tbsp fresh curly parsley, finely chopped (10 g)
- 2 eggs
- 1 tsp wheat germ

Nutrition Facts:
(Analytical components in 3.5 oz)

- **Recipe's kcal**   **115 kcal**
- Fat   12 g
- Carbohydrate   4.1 g
- Fiber   9 g
- Protein   14 g

Preparation:

1. Preheat the oven to 350°F.
2. Line a baking tray with parchment paper or a silicone baking mat.
3. Finely chop the spinach and parsley.
4. In a small bowl, combine the flour, spinach, parsley, pumpkin puree, and eggs. Stir the mixture well with a wooden spoon.
5. Mix in the wheat germ.
6. Gradually add more flour, a bit at a time, stirring well between each addition until the dough is formed.
7. Turn the dough out onto floured wax paper. Cover the dough with a second sheet of wax paper. Use a rolling pin to roll the dough out to approximately 1/4 inch thickness.
8. Cut the dough into desired shapes using a cookie cutter or sharp knife.
9. Bake the treats at 350°F for 30 - 35 minutes.
10. Remove the treats from the oven and allow them to cool completely.
11. Store the treats in an airtight container in the pantry for 5 - 7 days, or in the refrigerator for up to 10 days.

DENTAL CARE & SENSITIVE DOG TREATS

Try these recipes if your pup has special needs but you don't want to skimp on the yum factor! These treats are a dream come true for dogs with sensitive tummies or those in need of a little extra dental care. We've whipped up gluten-free goodies that are gentle on digestion and free from allergy triggers. Plus, for our furry friends with dental concerns or those moments of not-so-fresh breath, we've got just the thing.

PUMPKIN & OATS TREAT

Ingredients:

- 2/3 cup pumpkin puree
  (sugar-free, unflavored) (100 g)
- 2 tbs peanut butter
  (Xylitol-free peanut butter)
- 2 large eggs
- 4 cup oat flour (500 g)
- 1/4 tsp rosehip powder (optional)

Nutrition Facts:
(Analytical components in 3.5 oz)

- **Recipe's kcal** **296 kcal**
- Fat   9.9 g
- Carbohydrate   41.4 g
- Fiber   4.4 g
- Protein   11.8 g

Preparation:

1. Prepare ingredients at room temperature.
2. Preheat the oven to 338 F (170° C), line the baking tray with parchment paper.
3. Mix the ingredients with a food blender to get a homogeneous "dough". Adjust amounts if needed.
4. Cover the bowl with cling film and put the mixture in the fridge for 20-25 minutes.
5. Sprinkle oat flour on a rolling board and roll the mixture.
6. Cut treats with knife or cookie cutters and bake for approximately 20 minutes, until golden brown.
7. Put them on a rack to cool completely.
8. Store in an airtight container or put them in the freezer to make them last longer.

SIMPLE PEANUT BUTTER TREAT

Ingredients:

- 9.2 oz oat flour (260 g)
- 4 tbsp peanut butter
  (Xylitol-free peanut butter) (60 g)
- 3 medium eggs
  1/5 cup water/bone broth (50 g)

trition Facts:
lytical components in 3.5 oz)

- ecipe's kcal   **115 kcal**
- t   12 g
- rbohydrate   4.1 g
- er   9 g
- tein   14 g

Preparation:

1. Preheat the oven to 350°F.
2. Line a baking tray with parchment paper or a silicone baking mat.
3. Finely chop the spinach and parsley.
4. In a small bowl, combine the flour, spinach, parsley, pumpkin puree, and eggs. Stir the mixture well with a wooden spoon.
5. Mix in the wheat germ.
6. Gradually add more flour, a bit at a time, stirring well between each addition until the dough is formed.
7. Turn the dough out onto floured wax paper. Cover the dough with a second sheet of wax paper. Use a rolling pin to roll the dough out to approximately 1/4 inch thickness.
8. Cut the dough into desired shapes using a cookie cutter or sharp knife.
9. Bake the treats at 350°F for 30 - 35 minutes.
10. Remove the treats from the oven and allow them to cool completely.
11. Store the treats in an airtight container in the pantry for 5 - 7 days, or in the refrigerator for up to 10 days.

CHICKEN & SWEET POTATO TREAT

Ingredients:

- 7 oz brown rice flour (200 g)
- 3.5 oz chicken breast (cooked, mashed) (100 g)
- 3.5 oz sweet potato (cooked, mashed) (100 g)
- 3 medium eggs
- 1/4 tsp turmeric (optional)

Preparation:

1. Prepare ingredients at room temperature.
2. Preheat the oven to 365 F (185° C), line the baking tray with parchment paper.
3. Beat the eggs, then mix the ingredients in a bowl to get a homogeneous "dough". Adjust amounts if needed.
4. Spread the mixture evenly on the baking tray, and bake for 30-40 minutes, until golden brown.
5. Put on a rack to cool completely. Break into pieces.
6. Store in an airtight container or put them in the freezer to make them last longer.

Nutrition Facts:
(Analytical components in 3.5 oz)

- **Recipe's kcal** — **205 kcal**
- Fat — 3.5 g
- Carbohydrate — 31.7 g
- Fiber — 2.3 g
- Protein — 11 g

BEEF AND SWEET POTATO BALLS

Ingredients:

- 1 cup cooked beef (225 g)
- 1 cup cooked sweet potatoes, mashed (225 g)
- 1/4 cup fresh curly parsley, chopped (7 g)

Preparation:

1. Preheat your oven to 350°F (175°C). Line a baking sheet with parchment paper for easy cleanup.
2. In a mixing bowl, combine the cooked beef, mashed sweet potatoes, and chopped parsley.
3. Mix the ingredients well until thoroughly combined. Then, roll the mixture into small balls, each about 1 inch in diameter, suitable fo dog to eat.
4. Place the formed balls on the prepared baking sheet, spacing the out evenly.
5. Bake in the preheated oven for about 15-20 minutes, or until t balls are firm and cooked through.
6. After baking, allow the beef and sweet potato balls to cool d safe temperature before serving to your dog.

Nutrition Facts:
(Analytical components in 3.5 oz)

- **Recipe's kcal** — **322 kcal**
- Fat — 13 g
- Carbohydrate — 35.6 g
- Fiber — 3.9 g
- Protein — 13.8 g

Nu (An

- *F*
- *F*
- *C*
- *Fil*
- *Pr*

YOGURT & BACON DOG BISCUITS

Ingredients:

- 8.8 oz oat flour (250 g)
- 1 large eggs
- 3.5 oz yogurt (plain, unsweetened) (100 g)
- 1.7 oz bacon (diced) (50 g)

Preparation:

1. Prepare ingredients at room temperature.
2. Preheat the oven to 338 F (170° C), line the baking tray with parchment paper.
3. Mix the ingredients in a bowl to get a homogeneous "dough". Adjust amounts if needed.
4. Sprinkle oat flour on a rolling board and roll the mixture.
5. Cut treats with knife or cookie cutters, and bake for approximately 20 minutes, until golden brown.
6. Put them on a rack to cool completely.
7. Store in an airtight container or put them in the freezer to make them last longer.

Nutrition Facts:
(Analytical components in 3.5 oz)

Recipe's kcal	**295 kcal**
Fat	10.1 g
Carbohydrate	36.6 g
Fiber	3.5 g
Protein	14.2 g

SENSITIVE STOMACH DOG TREATS

Ingredients:

- 3 cups old-fashioned rolled oats (250 g)
- 1 cup pumpkin puree (225 g)
- 2 large eggs

Preparation:

1. Preheat your oven to 350°F.
2. Line a baking sheet with parchment paper and set aside.
3. In a mixing bowl, combine the rolled oats, pumpkin puree, and eggs. Mix well until the ingredients form a ball of dough.
4. You can roll the dough out on a floured surface and use cookie cutters or a pizza cutter to create shapes. Alternatively roll the dough into small balls (using about 1 tablespoon) and place them on the prepared baking sheet.
5. Remember that these treats add to your dog's daily caloric intake. Avoid making the treats too large.
6. Bake the treats for about 20 minutes or until they turn golden brown.

Nutrition Facts:
(Analytical components in 3.5 oz)

Recipe's kcal	**185 kcal**
Fat	10.1 g
Carbohydrate	30.6 g
Fiber	5.5 g
Protein	7.2 g

GRAIN FREE CHICKPEA DOG TREATS

Ingredients:

- 1 cup chickpea flour (140 g)
- 1/2 cup plain unsweetened applesauce (115 g)
- 2 tbsp peanut butter (Xylitol-free peanut butter) (30 g)
- 1/4 cup stone-ground oats (optional) (30 g)

Nutrition Facts:
(Analytical components in 3.5 oz)

Recipe's kcal	**205 kcal**	
Fat	3.5 g	
Carbohydrate	31.7 g	
Fiber	2.3 g	
Protein	11 g	

Preparation:

1. Preheat your oven to 350 degrees Fahrenheit.
2. In a large bowl, mix the chickpea flour, applesauce and peanut butter together until well combined.
3. Roll the dough to a thickness of about 1/4 inch. Dust the board with additional chickpea flour or a sprinkle of steel-cut oats for visual contrast (if not strictly sticking to grain-free).
4. Use your favorite cookie cutters to cut out the dog biscuits. Place them on a parchment-lined cookie sheet.
5. Bake the cookies for 22 minutes or until they are just golden brown around the edges.
6. For a crunchier cookie, turn off the oven but leave the baking sheets inside. Keep an eye on them to ensure they don't over-brown.
7. Allow the treats to cool, then store them in an airtight container for longer shelf life.

GREEN BREATH REFRESHER TREAT

Ingredients:

- 1 cup spinach (225 g)
- 1/4 cup curly parsley (15 g)
- 1/4 cup plain low-fat yogurt (65 g)
- 6 fresh mint leaves

Preparation:

1. In a blender, combine the spinach, curly parsley, yogurt, and fresh mint leaves. Blend until the mixture is smooth. Add a splash of water if necessary to help get things moving.
2. Place silicone dog treat molds on a flat plate or baking sheet for easy transfer. Pour the mixture into the silicone molds, leaving a little room at the top for expansion during freezing.
3. Freeze the molds until the treats are solid, which should take about 4 hours.
4. Once frozen, pop the treats out of the molds and serve them as occasional treats for your dog.

Nutrition Facts:
(Analytical components in 3.5 oz)

Recipe's kcal	**165 kcal**	
Fat	5.5 g	
Carbohydrate	20.7 g	
Fiber	17.3 g	
Protein	11 g	

DENTAL DOG CHEWS

Ingredients:

- 1 cup bone broth (240 ml)
- 4 tbsp Gelatin
- 2 tbsp dried mint
- 1/2 cup ground bones (optional) (120 g)

Nutrition Facts:
(Analytical components in 3.5 oz)

Recipe's kcal	**165 kcal**
Fat	5.5 g
Carbohydrate	20.7 g
Fiber	17.3 g
Protein	11 g

Preparation:

1. In a saucepan, warm the broth over low to medium heat.
2. Add the gelatin to the broth, stirring until it's completely dissolved.
3. Once it starts to boil, reduce the heat to low. Stir in the dried mint and let it steep for about 5-10 minutes.
4. If using, add ground bone and mix thoroughly. Continue to simmer on low for 15-30 minutes, depending on your desired chew consistency (longer for harder chews).
5. Pour the mixture into silicone ice cube trays and place in the refrigerator to chill.
6. Keep the chews refrigerated.

Storage and Tips:

- Ground bones can be made using a meat grinder attachment on a Mixer. Unused ground bones can be frozen for later use.
- These chews are not only good for your dog's teeth but also provide joint support due to the gelatin content.

CHEWS & STRESS-RELIEF TREATS

Let's dive into a chew-tastic experience! These homemade goodies are a healthier, more affordable alternative to commercial dog chews. Made with natural ingredients like zucchini and carrots, they're packed with vitamins and fiber, perfect for your dog's digestion and overall health. Satisfying your pup's chewing instincts, they are sure to love every healthy bite!

VEG DOG CHEWS

Ingredients:

- 1 large zucchini
- 2 tsp. olive oil
- 1 tsp cinnamon
- 1 tsp turmeric

Nutrition Facts:
(Analytical components in 3.5 oz)

Recipe's kcal	**49 kcal**	
Fat	0.1 g	
Carbohydrate	0.9 g	
Fiber	4.9 g	
Protein	1.1 g	

Preparation:

1. Preheat the oven to 200° F.
2. Slice the zucchini into about 1/8" thick slices, ensuring they are no more than 1/4" thick. The thicker the slices, the longer they will take to dehydrate.
3. Line a baking sheet with parchment paper or aluminum foil for easy cleanup.
4. Lay the zucchini slices flat on the baking sheet.
5. Brush each slice with olive oil, then lightly sprinkle with cinnamon and turmeric.
6. Bake the chews for about 4-6 hours. Check after four hours; if they're not dried out enough, continue baking until all moisture is removed.
7. For dogs with dental issues, you can leave the chews a bit chewy to make them easier to eat.

CARROT DOG CHEWS

Ingredients:

- 10 whole carrots
- 4 cup bone or beef broth (900 g)

Nutrition Facts:
(Analytical components in 3.5 oz)

Recipe's kcal	**53 kcal**	
Fat	0.1 g	
Carbohydrate	0.9 g	
Fiber	5.9 g	
Protein	1.1 g	

Preparation:

1. Place the carrots in a large, wide pot. Pour in the broth and add enough water to cover the carrots. Bring the mixture to a boil, then cover the pot. Let the carrots cook until they are tender, which should take about 20 to 30 minutes.
2. Once cooked, place the carrots on a parchment-lined plate in a single layer. Freeze them until they are solid, which will take about 2 hours.
3. Serve these frozen carrot chews to your dog under supervision as an occasional treat. They can be a refreshing snack, especially on warm days.
4. Store any leftover carrot chews in an airtight container in the freezer.

Storage and Tips:

- Ensure the bone broth used is safe for dogs. It should not contain onions, garlic, excessive salt, or added seasonings.
- Monitor your dog while they enjoy these treats, especially if serving them frozen, to ensure they don't pose a choking hazard.
- These treats are a great way to provide hydration and nutrition while also offering a fun, crunchy experience for your dog.

EASY SWEET POTATO DOG CHEWS

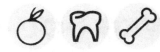

Ingredients:

- 2 sweet potatoes

Nutrition Facts:
(Analytical components in 3.5 oz)

- **Recipe's kcal** **60 kcal**
- Fat 0.1 g
- Carbohydrate 2.9 g
- Fiber 3.9 g
- Protein 1.1 g

Preparation:

1. Preheat your oven to 250°F (130°C). Line two baking sheets with parchment paper.
2. Use a knife or mandoline to slice the sweet potatoes. If you have a small dog, slice them into coin shapes. For larger dogs, you can slice the potatoes lengthwise for bigger chews. Aim for a thickness of no less than 1/4 inch to ensure they don't just become crispy but retain some chewiness.
3. Place the sweet potato slices in a single layer on the prepared baking sheets.
4. Bake the slices for 2 1/2 to 3 hours, flipping them once halfway through the baking time. They should be shrunken, dried out, and some pieces might be a bit crispy while others are chewier.
5. Allow the sweet potato chews to cool completely. Store them in an air-tight container in the refrigerator for up to 3 weeks.

HIMALAYAN CHEWS

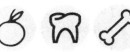

Ingredients:

- 1 gallon skim milk (4 lt)
- 1/2 cup lime juice (120 ml)
- 1 tsp Himalayan salt

Preparation:

1. Pour the skim milk into a large pot and heat it on low to medium heat. Bring it to a boil, stirring continuously.
2. Once the milk is boiling, turn off the heat. Add the lime juice and Himalayan salt, and stir gently for about 1-2 minutes, or until you see the whey begin to separate from the curd.
3. Allow the milk to sit undisturbed for 10-15 minutes.
4. Drape a cheesecloth or a clean dish towel over a large bowl. Drain the liquid, leaving only the curds in the cloth.
5. Twist the cheesecloth and squeeze out as much moisture as possible (the more moisture removed, the harder the treats will be).
6. Place the cheese still in the cheesecloth between books or weights, applying pressure for at least 4-6 hours.
7. Once pressed, remove the cheesecloth and cut the cheese into the desired size pieces.
8. Preheat the oven to 150°F. Bake the pieces for 40 minutes.
9. Spread the baked pieces on a cooling rack and let them dry for at least 24 hours.

Storage and Tips:

- This recipe uses lime juice instead of vinegar, which is safer for dogs.
- If you have a dehydrator, you can use it to speed up the drying process. Place the chews in the dehydrator at 150°F for 12-18 hours, turning them halfway through.
- Store the chews in airtight containers in a cool, dry, dark place. If there's a lot of moisture left, store them in the fridge for a longer shelf life.

Nutrition Facts:
(Analytical components in 3.5 oz)

- **Recipe's kcal** **53 kcal**
- Fat 0.1 g
- Carbohydrate 0.9 g
- Fiber 5.9 g
- Protein 1.1 g

TRIPE DOG CHEWS

Ingredients:

- 32 oz white tripe (1 kg)

Nutrition Facts:
(Analytical components in 3.5 oz)

- **Recipe's kcal** **110 kcal**
- Fat   5.9 g
- Carbohydrate 0.9 g
- Fiber   0.1 g
- Protein   15.1 g

Preparation:

1. Preheat your oven to 325 degrees Fahrenheit and line a cookie sheet with parchment paper.
2. Remove the tripe from its packaging and give it a thorough rinse.
3. Divide the tripe into two equal portions. Freeze one portion for future use.
4. Using a sharp knife or kitchen shears, cut the tripe with the grain into chew-size strips.
5. Bake the tripe strips for 90 minutes.
6. After the initial baking, flip over the chews on the cookie sheet and return them to the oven for an additional 30 minutes.
7. Allow the chews to cool before serving them to your dog.
8. Refrigerate the cooled chews for up to one week or store them in the freezer for longer preservation.

Storage and Tips:

- Ensure the tripe is cleaned properly before baking to ensure it's safe for your dog to consume.
- Monitor the baking process closely, as oven temperatures can vary and may affect the cooking time.

BLUEBERRY FROZEN DOG TREATS

Ingredients:

- 1 cup unsweetened plain greek yogurt (250 g)
- 1/2 cup blueberries (fresh, freeze-dried, or frozen) (80 g)
- Half a ripe banana, mashed
- Dog treat silicone molds (or ice cube trays)

Nutrition Facts:
(Analytical components in 3.5 oz)

- **Recipe's kcal** **90 kcal**
- Fat   0.9 g
- Carbohydrate 0.9 g
- Fiber   1.1 g
- Protein   10.1 g

Preparation:

1. Start by pureeing the blueberries in a blender. This step is crucial for creating a smooth texture and eliminating potential choking hazards, particularly for smaller dogs.
2. In a bowl, thoroughly mix the pureed blueberries, mashed banana, and greek yogurt until well combined.
3. Spoon or pour the mixture into your chosen dog treat molds. If preparing these treats for larger dogs. Place the filled molds in the freezer and freeze until the treats are solid.
4. Once frozen, pop the treats out of the molds. If you're using a muffin tin, you might need to briefly dip the bottom in warm water to help release the treats. Store the frozen treats in a freezer bag for up to three months.

Storage and Tips:

- Opt for a lower-fat version for weight management and always avoid sugar-added dried blueberries
- You might consider using larger molds like silicone baking cups or a muffin tin.

SUPERFOOD TREATS

'Superfood Treats' are packed with the essential nutrients of superfoods. From sweet potatoes and watermelon to spirulina and quinoa, each recipe is a nutritional powerhouse, ideal for enhancing your dog's health. With ingredients like turmeric for inflammation, fish oil for omega-3, and blueberries for antioxidants, these treats are not just delicious; they're incredibly beneficial. They're the perfect way to enrich your dog's diet while ensuring they relish every single bite!

FROZEN SPIRULINA CUBE

Ingredients:

- 2 cup bone broth (500 g)
- 1 tsp spirulina powder

Preparation:

1. Prepare ingredients at room temperature.
2. Mix spirulina powder into the bone broth.
3. Pour mixture into ice trays or freezer-safe silicone mold and freeze.

Nutrition Facts:
(Analytical components in 3.5 oz)

- **Recipe's kcal**   **16 kcal**
- Fat   0.1 g
- Carbohydrate   0.2 g
- Fiber   0 g
- Protein   3.8 g

DOG PROTEIN JELLY

Ingredients:

- 3 tbsp unflavored, unsweetened gelatin
- 5 tbsp (45 g) broth
- 1 tbsp (15 g) fresh applesauce for cooking or water
- 1/2 tsp spirulina powder

Preparation:

1. Add natural, plain, unflavored, unsweetened gelatin to cold broth
2. Let the gelatin "bloom" for a few minutes in the cold liquid.
3. Pour approximately 1 tbsp (15 g) applesauce (or water) into a bowl and bring it to a boil in the microwave oven.
4. Add bloomed gelatin to the hot liquid and mix thoroughly. Add spirulina powder.
5. Pour the mixture into a silicone mold or ice tray.
6. Put the mold/ice tray into the fridge for at least 2-3 hours until the mixture sets.
7. Keep jelly treats in the fridge, especially on hot summer days.

Nutrition Facts:
(Analytical components in 3.5 oz)

- **Recipe's kcal**   **90 kcal**
- Fat   0.1 g
- Carbohydrate   0.2 g
- Fiber   0.4 g
- Protein   42 g

BLACK CHARCOAL TREAT

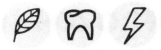

Ingredients:

- 1/2 cup unsweetened applesauce (115 g)
- 1/3 cup coconut milk (75 g)
- 1 Egg
- 1 tbsp melted coconut oil
- 1 1/2 cups brown rice flour or oat flour (220 g)
- 2 tbsp activated charcoal powder
- 1/2 cup chopped fresh curly parsley (30 g)

Nutrition Facts:
(Analytical components in 3.5 oz)

- **Recipe's kcal**   **170 kcal**
- Fat   8.9 g
- Carbohydrate   5.9 g
- Fiber   3.1 g
- Protein   9.1 g

Preparation:

1. Preheat the oven to 350°F.
2. In a medium bowl, mix the applesauce, coconut milk, egg, and melted coconut oil together.
3. Add the brown rice flour (or oat flour), activated charcoal powder, and chopped parsley to the wet ingredients. Stir until a dough forms.
4. Press the dough into a silicone tray with the mold shapes of your choice.
5. Bake the treats for 20 to 25 minutes.
6. After baking, remove the treats from the mold and let them cool on a wire rack.
7. Store the cooled treats in an airtight container in the refrigerator.

Storage and Tips:

- For a rollable dough that you can cut into shapes, add an additional 1/2 to 1 cup of flour and one more tablespoon of charcoal powder.

WATERMELON PUPSICLES

Ingredients:

- 1 1/2 cups fresh seedless watermelon pieces (160 g)
- 2/3 cup plain greek yogurt (160 g)
- 2 tsp honey

Nutrition Facts:
(Analytical components in 3.5 oz)

- **Recipe's kcal**   **116 kcal**
- Fat   1.9 g
- Carbohydrate   4.2 g
- Fiber   6 g
- Protein   4.1 g

Preparation:

1. Place silicone molds on a baking sheet to facilitate easy transfer to the freezer.
2. In a food processor, blend the watermelon pieces, greek yogurt, and honey until the mixture is smooth.
3. Pour the blended mixture into a measuring cup with a spout for convenience.
4. Carefully fill each slot of the silicone molds to the top with the watermelon mixture.
5. Freeze the molds for about 3 hours or until the mixture is solid.
6. Once frozen, gently release the pupsicles from the molds and offer them to your dog.

Storage and Tips:

- Silicone molds are recommended for ease of use. These treats are small-sized, suitable for all dog sizes. For larger dogs, consider using bigger molds or adjusting the serving size.
- Honey is generally safe for dogs in small amounts, but avoid it for puppies, dogs with compromised immune systems, obesity, or diabetes.

TURMERIC DOGGY TREAT

Ingredients:

- 1 cup oat flour (90 g)
- 1 cup chickpea flour (90 g)
- 3 tbsp turmeric (ground)
- 1 tbsp ground flax seed
- 2/3 cup peanut butter (Xylitol-free peanut butter) (100 g)
- 1/4 cup water (60 ml)

Nutrition Facts:
(Analytical components in 3.5 oz)

- **Recipe's kcal**   **160 kcal**
- Fat   10.1 g
- Carbohydrate   5.2 g
- Fiber   3 g
- Protein   4.8 g

Preparation:

1. Preheat your oven to 350°F.
2. In a large mixing bowl, combine the oat flour, chickpea flour, ground turmeric, ground flax seed, peanut butter, and water.
3. Mix the ingredients until the mixture becomes crumbly.
4. Form the mixture into two large balls and roll them out.
5. Use cookie cutters to cut the dough into various shapes.
6. Place the cutouts onto a prepared baking sheet.
7. Bake in the oven for 25 minutes. Then, turn off the oven but leave the treats inside for an additional 10-15 minutes or until they become crisp.
8. Once done, remove from the oven and let them cool.

QUINOA DOGGY TREATS

Ingredients:

- 2 1/2 cups quinoa flour (300 g)
- 1/4 cup flax seed meal (30 g)
- 1/2 cup bone broth (120 ml)
- 1 ripe banana
- 1 egg

Nutrition Facts:
(Analytical components in 3.5 oz)

- **Recipe's kcal**   **130 kcal**
- Fat   5.1 g
- Carbohydrate   9.2 g
- Fiber   5 g
- Protein   12.8 g

Preparation:

1. Preheat your oven to 350°F and line cookie sheets with parchment paper.
2. In a small bowl, mash the banana thoroughly.
3. In a larger bowl, combine the quinoa flour, flaxseed meal, egg, and mashed banana. Stir until well mixed.
4. Gradually add the bone broth mixture to the flour mixture. Add small amounts at a time until a pliable dough is formed.
5. Roll out the dough to a thickness of 1/4 to 1/2 inch. Use cookie cutters to cut into shapes and place them on the prepared cookie sheets.
6. Bake in the preheated oven for 20 to 23 minutes.
7. Remove from the oven and let the treats cool on racks.
8. Store the cooled treats in airtight containers in the refrigerator or freezer for longer preservation.

Storage and Tips:

- If the dough isn't at the desired consistency, adjust by adding small amounts of either flour or water, and blend together until you achieve a pliable dough.
- Quinoa Treats are not only gluten-free but also high in protein, making them a nutritious option for your furry friend.

HOLIDAY & SPECIAL OCCASION TREATS

If you enjoy whipping up something sweet, this section is for you and your furry friend. From birthdays to holidays and every special moment in between, these dog-friendly desserts are perfect for making your canine companion feel like a cherished part of the family. Each treat is crafted to bring joy and make them feel loved and super special on their big days. Dive in and discover delightful ways to include your pup in every celebration!

FAKE CHOCOLATE TRUFFLES

Ingredients:

- 3 large tbsp coconut oil
- 1 tbsp carob powder
- 4-5 strawberries (fresh or frozen)
- 1/2 tsp spirulina powder
- silicone baking molds or ice cube tray

Nutrition Facts:
(Analytical components in 3.5 oz)

Recipe's kcal	**110 kcal**
Fat	5.1 g
Carbohydrate	6.2 g
Fiber	5 g
Protein	4.8 g

Preparation:

1. Gently warm 2 tablespoons of coconut oil over low heat. Add the carob powder and mix until it's fully incorporated.
2. Spoon the carob mixture into the bottom of each mold, using about 1/2 tablespoon per mold. Place the molds in the freezer for 20 minutes to set the carob layer.
3. While the carob layer is chilling, puree the strawberries in a food processor or blender until they reach an ice-cream-like consistency.
4. Spoon the blended strawberries over the set carob layer in the molds. Return to the freezer for another 20 minutes.
5. Warm the last tablespoon of coconut oil in a pan. Stir in the spirulina powder and mix well.
6. Pour the spirulina mixture over the chilled strawberry layer in each mold to create a third layer.
7. Place the molds back in the freezer until the truffles are completely set.

Storage and Tips:

- These 'Fake Chocolate Truffles' are a dog-safe treat that mimics the layered look of traditional truffles. Carob is used as a safe alternative to chocolate.
- Spirulina adds a nutritious touch to these treats, but it's important to use it in moderation.

FAKE RED CHOCOLATE TRUFFLES

Ingredients:

- 1 large beet
- 1/2 cup coconut flour (60 g)
- 1/2 cup unsweetened shredded coconut (35 g)
- 3 tbsp carob chips
- 2 tbsp peanut butter (Xylitol-free peanut butter) (30 g)

Nutrition Facts:
(Analytical components in 3.5 oz)

Recipe's kcal	**110 kcal**
Fat	5.1 g
Carbohydrate	6.2 g
Fiber	5 g
Protein	4.8 g

Preparation:

1. Peel and cut the beet into cubes, then boil for about 15 minutes until the beet can be easily pierced with a knife.
2. Drain the water and puree the boiled beet in a blender until smooth. You should get approximately 3/4 cup of beet puree.
3. Add carob chips to the warm beet puree and blend until the chips melt and the mixture becomes smooth.
4. Pour the beet and carob mixture into a bowl. Stir in the peanut butter and coconut flour until well combined.
5. Roll the mixture into bite-sized balls.
6. Roll each ball in shredded coconut to coat it evenly.
7. Place the treats in the refrigerator for about 20 minutes or until they become firm.

Storage and Tips:

- 'Fake Chocolate Truffles' are a dog-safe treat that mimics the layered look of traditional truffles. Carob is used as a safe alternative to chocolate.
- This recipe creates healthy and appealing treats that are perfect for rewarding your dog or for special occasions.

DOG PUMPKIN TRUFFLES

Ingredients:

- 2 cups rolled oats (180 g)
- 1/3 cup shredded, unsweetened coconut flakes (30 g)
- 1/3 cup peanut butter (Xylitol-free peanut butter) (85 g)
- 1/3 cup canned pumpkin puree (75 g)
- 1 tbsp coconut oil

Preparation:

1. Place the shredded coconut in a bowl and set it aside for later use.
2. In a food processor or blender, add the rolled oats, unsweetened peanut butter, canned pumpkin puree, and coconut oil.
3. Pulse the ingredients a few times on high for about 30 seconds each time. Continue until you achieve a crumbly mixture.
4. Take 1 tablespoon portions of the mixture and roll them into balls.
5. Roll each ball in the coconut flakes until evenly coated.
6. Store the dog truffles in an airtight container in the refrigerator.

Nutrition Facts:
(Analytical components in 3.5 oz)

- **Recipe's kcal**   **176 kcal**
- Fat   5.7 g
- Carbohydrate   10 g
- Fiber   12 g
- Protein   7.8 g

HAM & EGG PUDDING

Ingredients:

- 5 large eggs
- 5.3 oz ham (chopped) (150 g)
- 7 oz yogurt (unsweetened, unflavored) (200 g)

Preparation:

1. Preheat oven to 320 F (160° C)
2. Mix all ingredients in a large bowl until fully combined.
3. Spray muffin tin or oven-safe silicone mold with coconut oil.
4. Fill cups ¾ way and bake until the mixture is fully set (approximately 15-20 minutes, depending on the oven).
5. Let it cool down completely, remove pudding with a spatula.
6. Store in the fridge in an airtight container to make them last longer.

Nutrition Facts:
(Analytical components in 3.5 oz)

- **Recipe's kcal**   **116 kcal**
- Fat   5.7 g
- Carbohydrate   3 g
- Fiber   0 g
- Protein   12.8 g

BEETROOT PANCAKE

Ingredients:

- 4.2 oz beetroot (cooked) (120 g)
- 0.7 oz blueberries (20 g)
- 2.1 oz yogurt (unsweetened, unflavored) (60 g)
- 3.5 oz brown rice flour (100 g)

Preparation:

1. Puree cooked beetroot and blueberries.
2. Mix ingredients in a blender or in a bowl until fully combined, set aside. Alternatively, you can use oat flour instead of brown rice flour.
3. Preheat a non-stick pan and fry pancakes until golden brown. You can use a teaspoon of coconut oil for frying to prevent sticking.
4. Let it cool down, and serve, or store in the fridge for 4-5 days or freeze pancakes to make them last longer.

Nutrition Facts:
(Analytical components in 3.5 oz)

- **Recipe's kcal**   **158 kcal**
- Fat   1.4 g
- Carbohydrate   7.2 g
- Fiber   2.5 g
- Protein   4.2 g

CHRISTMAS CINNAMON BONES

Ingredients:

- 2 cups whole-wheat flour (240 g)
- 1/2 cup unsweetened applesauce (120 g)
- 1/4 cup water (60 g)
- 1/2 tsp cinnamon

Preparation:

1. Preheat your oven to 350°F (175°C). Line a baking sheet with parchment paper.
2. In a mixing bowl, combine the whole wheat flour and cinnamon.
3. Add the applesauce and water to the dry ingredients.
4. Mix everything together until a dough forms.
5. On a lightly floured surface, roll out the dough to about 1/4 inch thickness.
6. Use a bone-shaped cookie cutter to cut out the treats, or shape them as desired.
7. Place the treats on the prepared baking sheet. Bake for about 20-25 minutes, or until they are firm and slightly browned.
8. Allow the treats to cool completely before serving to your dog.

Storage and Tips:

- Christmas Cinnamon Bones are a festive and healthy treat for your dog, perfect for the holiday season.
- The cinnamon not only adds flavor but is also known for its anti-inflammatory properties.

Nutrition Facts:
(Analytical components in 3.5 oz)

- **Recipe's kcal**   **116 kcal**
- Fat   5.7 g
- Carbohydrate   3 g
- Fiber   0 g
- Protein   12.8 g

BLUEBERRY COOKIES

Ingredients:

- 7 oz oat flour (200 g)
- 3 large eggs
- 1 tbsp salmon oil
- 3.5 oz blueberries (mashed) (100 g)
- 1/4 tsp rosehip powder (optional)

Preparation:

1. Prepare ingredients at room temperature.
2. Preheat the oven to 338 F (170° C), line the baking tray with parchment paper.
3. Mix the ingredients in a bowl to get a homogeneous "dough". Adjust amounts if needed.
4. Sprinkle oat flour on a rolling board and roll the mixture.
5. Cut treats with knife or cookie cutters, and bake for approximately 20 minutes, until golden brown.
6. Put them on a rack to cool completely.
7. Store in an airtight container or put them in the freezer to make them last longer.

Nutrition Facts:
(Analytical components in 3.5 oz)

- **Recipe's kcal**   **230 kcal**
- Fat   7,1 g
- Carbohydrate   32 g
- Fiber   3.4 g
- Protein   10.5 g

PEANUT BUTTER PUPCAKES

Ingredients:

- 1 cup whole-wheat flour (120 g)
- 1/4 cup peanut butter (Xylitol-free peanut butter) (65 g)
- 1/4 cup unsweetened applesauce (60 g)
- 1/4 cup grated carrots (40 g)
- 1/4 cup water (60 g)
- 1 tsp baking powder
- 1 egg

Preparation:

1. Preheat your oven to 350°F (175°C). Line a muffin tin with cupcake liners.
2. In a mixing bowl, combine the whole wheat flour and baking powder.
3. In a separate bowl, thoroughly mix the peanut butter, applesauce, grated carrots, water, and egg.
4. Gradually add the dry ingredients to the wet mixture, stirring until well combined.
5. Spoon the batter evenly into the cupcake liners in the muffin tin.
6. Bake the pupcakes for about 15-20 minutes, or until a toothpick inserted into the center comes out clean.
7. Allow the pupcakes to cool completely before serving them to your dog.

Nutrition Facts:
(Analytical components in 3.5 oz)

- **Recipe's kcal**   **214 kcal**
- Fat   6.8 g
- Carbohydrate   29.4 g
- Fiber   2.3 g
- Protein   9.7 g

CHICKEN PUPCAKES

Ingredients:

- 1 cup whole wheat flour (120 g)
- About 2.1 oz chicken breast (60 g)
- 1/4 cup olive oil (60 g)
- 2 eggs
- 2 tbsp peanut butter
  (Xylitol-free peanut butter) (30 g)

Nutrition Facts:
(Analytical components in 3.5 oz)

- **Recipe's kcal**   **230 kcal**
- Fat   7.8 g
- Carbohydrate   27.4 g
- Fiber   1.3 g
- Protein   19.7 g

Preparation:

1. Boil the chicken breast until it's fully cooked. Let it cool and then finely chop or blend it.
2. In a bowl, combine the olive oil and eggs.
3. Continue to mix while adding the chopped or blended chicken.
4. Gradually add the whole wheat flour, mixing it in with a spatula. If the dough seems too thick, add a tablespoon of milk to soften it.
5. Preheat your oven to 350°F (about 180°C).
6. Grease the muffin tins lightly with flour and fill them up to 3/4 full with the batter.
7. Bake the cupcakes for 10-15 minutes. Check for doneness with a toothpick—if it comes out clean, the cupcakes are ready.
8. Allow the cupcakes to cool completely, then decorate them with peanut butter and top with a dog treat for an extra special touch.

PUPCORN

Ingredients:

- 3 tbsp popcorn kernels
- 2 tbsp peanut butter
  (Xylitol-free peanut butter) (30 g)
- 1 tbsp honey
- A brown paper vegetable bag

Nutrition Facts:
(Analytical components in 3.5 oz)

- **Recipe's kcal**   **186 kcal**
- Fat   5.7 g
- Carbohydrate   9 g
- Fiber   11 g
- Protein   1.8 g

Preparation:

1. Place the popcorn kernels in a brown paper vegetable bag. Firmly close the bag by folding the top. Microwave the kernels at 900W for about 3-4 minutes or until the popping sound nearly stops. Remove and pour the popcorn into a bowl.
2. In a separate bowl, mix the peanut butter with the honey.
3. Drizzle the peanut butter and honey mixture over the popcorn. Stir thoroughly to evenly coat all the popcorn.
4. Spread the coated popcorn on a baking tray lined with parchment paper. Preheat the oven to 320°F (160°C) with the fan on, and bake for 10 minutes.
5. Allow the popcorn to cool down a bit before serving it to your dog.

Storage and Tips:

- PUPcorn is a fun and tasty treat for dogs, perfect for special occasions like movie nights. It's easy to make and can be enjoyed by both you and your furry friend!
- Popcorn is a source of potassium, magnesium, and calcium, beneficial for bones and the immune system.

CONCLUSION

So, here we are on the last page, the one with greetings and thanks.

The first goes to you, dear reader, for choosing to unconditionally love that wonderful furry creature that lives with you. For thousands of years, dogs and humans have lived side by side: from wolves that fed on leftovers together with hunters, to guide dogs that help people with disabilities and everything else. And as a result of this long history, today, most of us consider our dogs an integral part of the family. They are our best friends and we always want the best for them. We wish for a long and happy life together.

Thank you for being willing to invest your time to show them love and care.

Cooking for our dogs is a great way to bond even more closely with them, and in particular preparing small snacks, rewards, and sweets is an especially wholesome way to spoil them. Not only that, cooking treats also proves to be a moment of absolute relaxation and pleasure within the week, an activity that can also be educational if done as a family involving the youngest, a way to teach care and respect. And no one knows how to show appreciation and pure joy in front of your preparations as much as a dog. No criticism for an imperfect ball or a too dry cookie!

Seeing them wag their tails excitedly in front of their reward gives you the same joy, so the food you have prepared for them can be an even greater reward for you than it is for them.

I hope that you've found some delicious and healthy recipes in this book. I also hope that you've found some inspiration and joy. After all, that's what dogs are all about: they bring us joy and they teach us to love and care for others. They make the world a better place.

Thank you again for being a part of this journey. I wish you and your dog all the best.

Sincerely,

Jimi Foster

If you enjoyed this book and if the recipes contained in it have brought you joy, please consider writing a short review on Amazon. A small gesture for which I will be immensely grateful.

RECIPES CATEGORY INDEX

	Meat-Based	Fish-Based	Vegetarian	NO-Bake	Frozen	Training	Low-Fat	Dental Care	Sensitive	Chews & Stress Relief	Super Food	Special Occasion	Baking Mats	PAG.
Chicken Lover Treat	✓					✓	✓							17
Beef Dog Treat	✓					✓							✓	17
Lamb Dog Treat	✓					✓							✓	18
Lamb & Carrot Treat	✓					✓			✓					18
Cheddar & Bacon Delights	✓								✓			✓		19
Peanut Butter Bacon Dog Treats	✓								✓			✓		19
Tuna Dog Treat		✓					✓						✓	21
Salmon & Pumpkin Dog Treat		✓					✓						✓	21
Tuna & Carrot Dog Treat		✓				✓	✓							22
Salmon & Carrot Dog Treat		✓				✓			✓					22
Whitefish and Wild Rice Treats		✓					✓		✓					23
Peanut Butter & Broth Dog Biscuits		✓					✓						✓	23
Sweet & "Spicy" Chips			✓				✓			✓				25
Oat & Apple Treat			✓			✓	✓							25
Sweet Potato & Carrot Treat			✓			✓			✓					26
Pumpkin & Oats Treat			✓						✓				✓	26
Apple Carrot Biscuits			✓			✓						✓		27
Vegetable Turmeric Dog Treats			✓			✓						✓		28

Recipe	Protein	Leaf	✕	Frozen	Oval	Fruit	Gluten-Free	Bone	Lightning	Crown	Paw	Page
Overnight Oats for Dogs		🌿	✕				🌾̶					30
Fruit Mix Puree		🌿	✕			🍎						30
Banana Snowballs		🌿	✕							👑		31
Easy Pumpkin & Cinnamon Treats		🌿	✕							👑		31
Dog Pumpkin-Balls		🌿	✕				🌾̶					32
Bacon & Banana Snowballs	🍗		✕							👑		32
Overnight Oats & Fruits for Dogs		🌿	✕							👑		33
Banana Bites		🌿				🍎	🌾̶					35
Bacon & Pear	🍗						🌾̶			👑		35
PAWnut Butter Freeze Treats			✕	❄️							🐾	36
Pumpkin & Banana				❄️			🌾̶				🐾	36
Easy Sweet Potatoes Biscuits		🌿				🍎					🐾	38
Sardine Dog Biscuits	🐟						🌾̶		⚡			37
Frozen Banana		🌿		❄️							🐾	40
Peanut butter & Banana		🌿		❄️							🐾	40
Frozen Hen Soup				❄️		🍎					🐾	41
Berry Ice Cream		🌿		❄️							🐾	41
DOG Gummies				❄️		🍎				👑		42
Cantaloupe Ice Cream		🌿		❄️		🍎						42
Frozen Pumpkin Delight				❄️		🍎					🐾	43
Beef After Training Snack	🍗				🏈				⚡			45
Easy Training Treats	🍗				🏈		🌾̶					45
Light After Training Snack	🐟				🏈				⚡			46
Banana After Training Snack			✕		🏈			🦴				46

Treat	Protein	Leaf	X	Oval	Apple	Tooth	Grain-Free	Bone	Lightning	Crown	Paw	Page
Salmon Swirl Training Treats	🐟			⬭					⚡			47
Microwaved Hot Dog Training Treats	🍗			⬭			🌾̸					47
Tuna Soft Treats	🐟			⬭			🌾̸					48
Small Bite-Sized Rewards	🍗			⬭							🐾	48
Zucchini Light Chips		🍃			🍎		🌾̸					50
Boiled Egg Dog Treat			✕		🍎							50
Light Shrimp, Salmon Oil, and Apple Dog Treat	🐟						🌾̸			👑		51
Easy Low-Fat Biscuits		🍃			🍎		🌾̸					51
Low-Calorie Broth Doggy Treats	🍗				🍎		🌾̸					52
Tuna & Turmeric Dog Treat	🐟				🍎				⚡			52
Light Pumpkin & Banana		🍃			🍎						🐾	53
Low Calorie Pumpkin & Spinach Treats		🍃			🍎						🐾	53
Pumpkin & Oats Treat		🍃		⬭			🌾̸					55
Simple Peanut Butter Treat		🍃		⬭			🌾̸					55
Chicken & Sweet Potato Treat	🍗			⬭			🌾̸					56
Beef and Sweet Potato Balls	🍗						🌾̸			👑		56
Yogurt & Bacon Dog Biscuits	🍗			⬭			🌾̸					57
Sensitive Stomach Dog Treats		🍃		⬭			🌾̸					57
Grain Free Chickpea Dog Treats		🍃		⬭			🌾̸					58
Green Breath Refresher Treat		🍃				🦷					🐾	58
Dental Dog Chews						🦷		🦴			🐾	59
VEG Dog Chews						🦷		🦴	⚡			61
Carrot Dog Chews					🍎	🦷		🦴				61
Easy Sweet Potato Chews					🍎	🦷		🦴				62

Product	Meat	Leaf	No	Frozen	Apple	Tooth	Grain-free	Bone	Energy	Crown	Paw	Page
Himalayan Chews					🍎	🦷		🦴				62
Tripe Dog Chews	🍗					🦷		🦴				63
Blueberry Frozen Dog Treats						🦷		🦴	⚡			63
Frozen Spirulina Cube				❄					⚡		🐾	65
Dog Protein Jelly			✕		🍎				⚡			65
Black Charcoal Treat		🍃				🦷			⚡			66
Watermelon PUPsicles				❄					⚡	👑		66
Turmeric Doggy Treat		🍃					⚕		⚡			67
Quinoa Doggy Treats					🍎		⚕		⚡			67
Fake Chocolate Truffles			✕							👑	🐾	69
Fake Red Chocolate Truffles			✕							👑	🐾	69
Dog Pumpkin Truffles		🍃	✕							👑		70
Ham & Egg Pudding	🍗									👑	🐾	70
Beetroot Pancake		🍃							⚡	👑		71
Christmas Cinnamon Bones		🍃							⚡	👑		71
Blueberry Cookies							⚕		⚡	👑		72
Peanut Butter PUPcakes		🍃								👑		72
Chicken PUPcakes	🍗									👑		73
PUPcorn			✕					🦴		👑		73

METRIC CONVERSION CHART

Oven Temperatures

NO FAN	FAN FORCED	FARENHEIT
120 °C	100 °C	250 °C
150 °C	130 °C	300 °C
160 °C	140 °C	325 °C
180 °C	160 °C	350°C
190 °C	170 °C	375°C
200 °C	180 °C	400°C
230 °C	210 °C	450°C
250 °C	230 °C	500°C

Sr Flour = Self Raising

Cup and Spoons

CUP	METRIC
1/4 cup	60 ml
1/3 cup	80 ml
1/2 cup	125ml
1 cup	250 ml
SPOONS	**SPOONS**
1/4 teaspoon	1.25 ml
1/2 teaspoon	2.5 ml
1 teaspoon	5 ml
2 teaspoon	10 ml
1 Tablespoon	20 ml

Liquids

Cup	Metric	Imperial
	30ml	1 fl oz
1/4 Cup	60ml	2 fl oz
1/3 Cup	80 ml	31/2 fl oz
	100 ml	23/4 fl oz
1/2 Cup	125 ml	4 fl oz
	150 ml	5 fl oz
3/4 Cup	180 ml	6 fl oz
	200 ml	7 fl oz
1 Cup	250 ml	83/4 fl oz
11/4 Cups	310 ml	101/2 fl oz
11/2 Cups	375 ml	13 fl oz
13/4 Cups	430 ml	15 fl oz
	475 ml	16 fl oz
2 Cups	500 ml	17 fl oz
21/2 Cups	625 ml	211/2 fl oz
3 Cups	750 ml	26 fl oz
4 Cups	1L	35 fl oz
5 Cups	1.25L	44 fl oz
6 Cups	1.5L	52 fl oz
8 Cups	2L	70 fl oz
10 Cups	2.5L	88 fl oz

Mass

Imperial	Metric
1/4 oz	10g
1/2 oz	15 g
1 oz	30 g
2 oz	60 g
3 oz	90 g
4 oz (1/4 lb)	125 g
5 oz	155 g
6 oz	185 g
7 oz	220 g
8 oz (1/2 lb)	250 g
9 oz	280 g
10 oz	315 g
11 oz	345 g
12 oz (3/4 lb)	375 g
13 oz	410 g
14 oz	440 g
15 oz	470 g
16 oz (1 lb)	500 g
24 oz (11/2 lb)	750 g
32 oz (2 lb)	1kg
48 oz (3 lb)	1.5kg

ALPHABETICAL INGREDIENTS INDEX

Printed in Great Britain
by Amazon

39477932R00051